30 March 1995

To My Friend
Al Fisher
    May you have many
happy days of Toy Soldiers
    in your retirement.

            John Sonner

Model Soldiers

Jack Cassin-Scott

Model Soldiers

B. T. Batsford Ltd, London

To my son, Tony

ISBN 0 7134 5950 6

Typeset by J&L Composition Ltd,
Filey, North Yorkshire
and printed in Great Britain by
The Bath Press
Bath
for the publishers
B. T. Batsford Ltd
4 Fitzhardinge Street
London W1H 0AH

Contents

1 General principles

Modelling in any medium is a process of building up, as opposed to sculpture, which involves chipping away or carving from a solid piece of material. If you are willing to set your sights high, and to learn a few basic rules, here is a satisfying hobby at your fingertips. The standard of proficiency you reach in modelling depends on the time, enthusiasm and amount of practice you are prepared to put into your work. Technique is important, but there are as many techniques as there are modellers. Each person will, in the course of time, create his or her own style. But, one has to start somewhere; you cannot formulate your own technique straight away. Remember you are attempting to create a model; follow the instructions in this book and let your technique look after itself.

Study your subjects well. Look at photographs, paintings, models, statues, and the people and animals around you. Read books on muscle and bone structure, and on anatomy in general. Do not get discouraged. The task set for you is not without its difficulties, as indeed it should not be, for the surmounting of these difficulties will make you more aware of the world around you. If you allow yourself to become more knowledgeable about nature and the wonderful things it has created, you will be a better modeller.

The general principles of all model-making methods are the same. First the model should be designed in some pliable material, for example clay, wax, Plasticine or other soft substance which has no permanence and can therefore be distorted easily. For the models in this book, you should use either clay or Plasticine as both work successfully. Clay, however, becomes dry if left, wax will melt with heat and Plasticine can easily be destroyed or damaged by accident. Once the preliminary model is made, therefore, it must be transferred into a more permanent material such as metal, plastic, resin, papier mâché, cement or latex composition. This is achieved by making a mould using various processes and materials which are described in detail in Chapter 3.

Learning how to handle and control your medium is most important. Whilst not underestimating the difficulties for a beginner faced with a lump of clay or Plasticine for the first time, I believe that modelling is a natural form of self-expression. As a child you probably played with Plasticine, making shapes and figures, and you need only to remind yourself of that creative ability. First of all, get the feel of the material. Roll it in your hands, knead it, squeeze it; make simple shapes such as cylinders, spheres and cubes. Gradually allow yourself to build bodies and faces, letting the fingers smooth shapes together. It is great fun and you

Left **1** Two British Grenadier 'Red Coats' of 1776 during the American War of Independence. *Latex composition, 30cm (12in)*

should enjoy it. Do not worry if your first results are disappointing; simply roll the material back into a ball and start again. Just practise, for this is the only way in which you will familiarize yourself with your modelling medium. At all stages of modelling remember these few points:

1 Make sure there is plenty of space around your table so that you can move around your work at will.
2 Always work at a height that suits you and at which you will feel comfortable for a considerable period of time.
3 If you use clay, keep the consistency just right; not too hard and not too soft.
4 Keep your tools within easy reach, and always make sure they are clean. There is nothing worse than picking up a tool to smooth in a little detail and finding it is covered in clay.
5 Use your hands at all times. They are your most important tools, and you should use your wooden spatula tools only for finer detail work and inaccessible places.
6 Use water sparingly. A dripping clay model becomes unworkable and fine detail simply disappears. A finger dipped in water is sufficient for smoothing off.
7 Check that you have good lighting, especially when you are modelling high-lights and shadows. Natural light is best, but if you are working in a studio use a top light set at 45 degrees.
8 If you work at home, make sure that you work in a place where you can leave your equipment and unfinished models for a period without inconvenience.

Tools and materials

This is a list of the basic equipment you will need to start all the types of modelling dealt with in this book.

1 *Modelling medium:*
- clay: you can buy this ready to use in 3kg (7lb) packs from any art shop. Keep it in a galvanized tin with a damp cloth over the top. The consistency is most important: if the clay is too hard, it will be difficult to work with, and if it is too soft it will be sticky and unmanageable.
- a polythene sheet to keep your work damp during clay modelling.
- Plasticine: this is a very useful modelling medium and I strongly recommend it for general practice. Although it is pliable in its natural state, you can make it a softer consistency if required by warming it. This will not cause any damage to the normal plasticity when it has cooled off. One great advantage is that it does not require damping. The model can be left for long periods of time without any protection, and will not crack or break up.
- papier mâché pulp: this is cheap and convenient for modelling.

2 *Modelling board*: a base of 30cm × 60cm (12in × 24in) made either from two thicknesses of flooring or one thickness battened on the underside with two pieces of wood to stop it warping.

3 *Modelling tools:*
- wooden spatulas: three or four of various sizes
- medium-sized wire-ended tool
- callipers

4 *Figure iron*: the adjustable type, available from art shops, is the most useful.

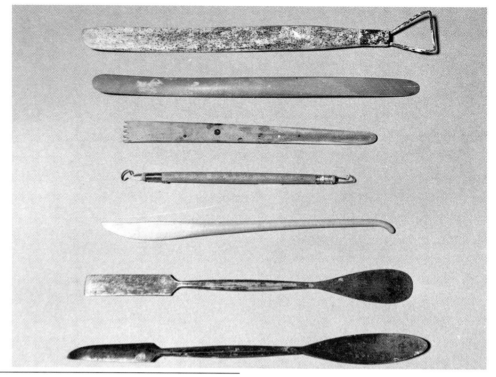

2 A selection of useful modelling tools.

3 Equipment for mixing and applying plaster of Paris.

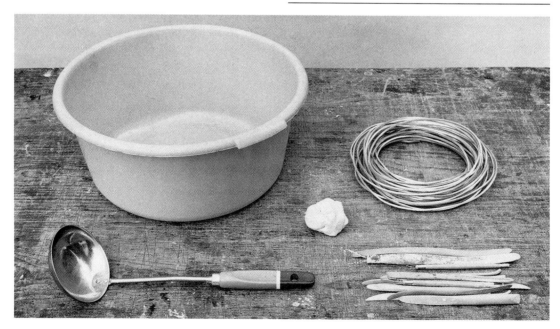

5 *Wire*: lead or square aluminium wire of about 5mm (³⁄₁₆in) gauge is sufficient. This is sold by weight, with approximately 1.3m per kg (23in per lb).

6 *Casting tools*:
- medium-sized flexible bowl for mixing in
- two metal spatulas for cleaning up the moulds
- one 2.5cm (1in) chisel
- several lengths of wood 15cm (6in) wide
- superfine plaster, available in bags of 25kg (55lb)
- several lengths of wood 15cm (6in) wide

There are many more materials that come in useful once in a while, but you can build up your collection gradually. The list opposite covers almost every possibility!

balsa wood	plaster rasp
block of metal	polystyrene glue
cold cure silicone rubber compound	rags for wiping
	razor blades
cold set solder	razor saw
craft knife and assorted blades	rasps
	sailmaker's needles
dividers	sandpaper, fine to flour
dowel sticks, various sizes	scissors
epoxy resin adhesive	scriber or engraver
fine chain	sharpening stone
fine saw	small hammer
glue size	small jars and tins
graphite powder	small set square
knitting needle	small trowel
latex composition	small vice
lead	solder
liquid detergent	soldering iron
liquid plastic and catalyst	steel ruler
	straight pins, various sizes
long-nosed pliers	
low-metal alloy	thin metal sheets
metal tubing, small diameter	turpentine or paint thinners
nails	tweezers
needle files	thread
paint brushes 000 to 3	Vinamold
	watchmaker's screwdriver
paints, water-based and enamel	water jug
palette of glass or porcelain	wire cutters
	wood for bases
pencil-type soldering iron	wooden mixing spoon
pencils	X-acto knife

4 An American paratrooper of 1944, wearing the full equipment including the 'Mae West' and the reserve parachute on the front.

To begin with you will find it an effort to command and control the materials and tools, but persevere and have confidence in your ability, and you will be amazed – and delighted – with the results you achieve.

2 Model kits

There are many soldier kits on the market today both in metal and plastic form. These come with assembly and painting instructions, and the finished product is very good. As well as the basic modelling tools listed in Chapter 1, you will find the following useful when assembling plastic and metal models from kits: a small metal cutting saw; a skiving knife for trimming; a cutting knife; metal files; and a watchmaker's screwdriver.

Assembly

The most important job for both types of kit is that all the pieces are there.

Metal kits

The first step when using a metal kit is to clean off the seam lines on each piece with a small file. Then see if all the pieces fit together, widening the neck and arm holes where necessary to ensure a good fit. Use an epoxy-resin adhesive to glue the kit together. Not only is this an excellent adhesive, but it acts as a filler as well, and by careful smoothing it obliterates any unseemly join lines. The glued pieces must be firmly held together. Any excess glue can be cut or filed off after it is dry. Fix the model to the base supplied, give the assembled figure a coat of metal primer and your model is ready for painting.

Plastic kits

The plastic kit takes a little more time because of the many pieces involved, but as each kit comes complete with well-drawn exploded diagrams, it is difficult to go astray. The first task is to see that everything is freed from the moulded tabs, then clean the flash lines and tab joining pieces. Join all the half pieces together – body, head, etc. As the plastic cement dries in minutes, it is always worthwhile checking that the arms, legs and head fit first.

Having checked that everything does fit perfectly, first attach the leg pieces to the body and then glue the feet firmly to the base. Apart from the actual sticking of the parts, you should now handle the model by holding the base only, especially during the painting operation. Next assemble the head and place it on the body. In most plastic kits there is a choice of arm positions, either at-ease or shoulder-arms; choose which one you think is best.

At this stage you can either continue to assemble the equipment or paint the basic uniform. If you decide to do the painting, a light wash over the model with a detergent will help prepare the surface. Also, make sure you use the correct paints for plastic. The final operation is the fitting of the equipment, which you can paint either before or after it is joined to the model. The latter is more difficult as the paint may overspill on the already-painted surface of the uniform. Either way your model is now complete. As you can see from pages 41–43, a latex composition model can also be made in parts, and the tools needed are similar to those already mentioned; the only extras are a tube of rubber-based adhesive and some sheets of fine sandpaper.

Converting

Most plastic kits consist of a variety of arms and equipment, allowing for a choice without animation, and some metal kits are in

5 Model kit of a British 'Brown Bess' rifle.

pieces allowing for a choice of arm movements. However, if you want to make a kit soldier fit your individual requirements, you will need to convert it.

Like every other aspect of model-soldier making, converting requires patience, practice and skill. The study of conversion is not without its pitfalls, and to create a model of your own choice from limited parts does demand a large amount of creative ability. To change a standing figure to a running position, for example, seems to be a simple problem, but you still have to decide where to cut, how deep to cut, and finally how to cut. These are important questions, so try to answer them before making even the smallest nick in your precious metal or plastic model soldier. The cost of converting could mean two or more models being cut up and stripped of various parts of equipment for

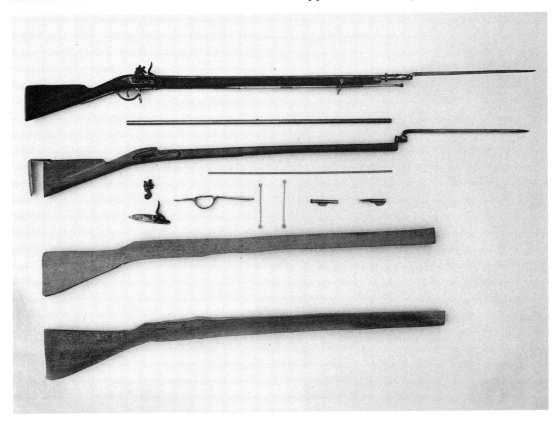

replanting. Think *before* dismantling the figures if the alterations you are contemplating improve the movement or if they make the figure look awkward.

The tools required for converting are the same as those required for making a master detailed figure (see page 11). As well as these, an electric pen soldering iron is very useful. Because of its many attachments, you can use it for both plastic and metal models. The 20-watt heating unit is fitted with several screw-on detachable heads. In plastic modelling, by placing the smallest head of the iron onto the inside of the arm you will make the plastic pliant enough to be bent into any position; legs can be treated in a like manner. Similarly, folds and crease lines can be retouched, bearskins can be remodelled and hair can be made to appear more dishevelled in action by applying the heated iron to the appropriate part.

Changing a figure

To bend a straight arm (or leg) on a metal model without using a soldering iron, cut a V-shaped notch on the inside of the elbow (or knee) part of the arm (or leg), then slowly bend it into the chosen position, remembering that the deeper the cut, the greater the animated action. A plastic arm is much easier: simply heat the cutting knife, cut a V-shape in the same position and fill in the gap by smoothing the knife over the join.

Astute combinations of figures with equipment can also make an enormous difference. You can use either some of the excellent kits (see fig. 5) or make individual items in the same way as for soldiers you have modelled yourself – see pages 47–59.

Changing a horse

Model horses can be converted by cutting up two or more into halves or quarters as necessary. Cut a V-shape just under the horse's head, which you can then twist either to one side or downward, whichever is better for your purpose (fig. 6). After positioning the head, fill the resulting gap with epoxy resin. Make reins from thin metal sheets or plastic strips, depending on the type of horse, cut to scale. Fine wire makes splendid manes and tails, giving the feeling of movement if you arrange it properly. Add a feeling of forward movement by bending the tassels and flounders, coat-tails and sabretaches in a backward direction. (See p. 51 for further details.)

6 Converting a horse's head position by cutting a V in the throat, then slowly turning or bending the head into the required position.

In the same way as kit soldiers can be improved by adding accessories, so too can horses, with the addition of bridles, for example. Bore a hole through the upper part of the horse's mouth and insert a fine wire, twisted into shape with a pair of long-nosed pliers (fig. 7).

Offcuts

You can make use of both plastic and metal offcuts resulting from conversions. Place any spare pieces from a metal model back in the melting pot for use on a future occasion. For plastic, you will need some carbon tetrachloride – you can buy this from a chemist but be careful, as it is an unpleasant chemical, so handle it with care. Pour some into a screw-top jar, add the pieces of sprue and plastic off-cuts and allow the ingredients to mix. Make sure that the lid of the jar is securely fastened, and allow the mixture to stand for a few hours. The solution turns into a liquid plastic and can be used to coat materials such as cloaks, crossbelts, reins, straps, etc.

For more detailed information of converting, consult any of the excellent specialist books in the bibliography on page 94.

7 Decorating a horse kit by boring a hole through the upper part of the horse's mouth and inserting a fine wire twisted into shape with a pair of long-nosed pliers.

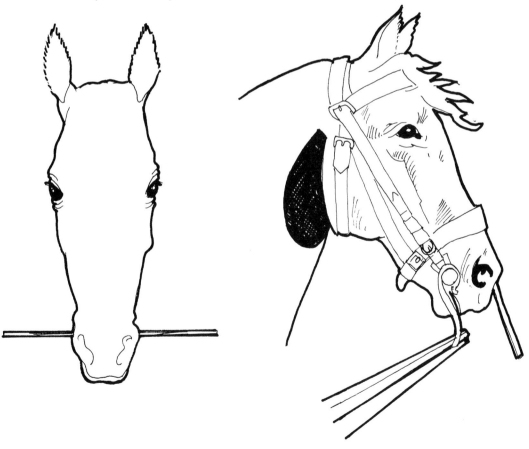

3 Modelling a figure

Before attempting to model a figure, work out with rough drawings the predetermined pose of your finished model, bearing in mind gravity and balance.

Large-scale models

The figure iron

Screw the figure iron (fig. 8a) to a wooden modelling board, about two-thirds up and a quarter in from the top right-hand corner. The support bar should be facing diagonally in the direction of the lower left-hand corner; this leaves plenty of space for laying on the clay (or Plasticine) base.

Place the horizontal support bar of the figure iron in a position where it can enter the back of your clay model just below the waist or roughly the centre of the figure (fig. 8b). The short arm, which is a movable extension of the horizontal bar, can be angled in any direction to give action to the model if necessary. For this model, I suggest you place the short arm in the upright position.

The armature

Now build a simple armature for a standing figure. A simple unit of measurement for the human body is the head. The average figure ranges from 6 to 7½ heads tall, and fig. 9 shows the relative proportions of the rest of the body to the head.

The armature should mirror as closely as possible the posture you have decided upon. Pull the arm wires away from the body armature for the time being to allow for easier modelling of the body. They can be bent back into position when you are ready to model them.

With the armature erected, lay a base large enough to accommodate the figure and about 25mm (1in) thick. When the base is cut away it will form the pouring holes through the feet of the figure. Make sure the leg armature is buried in the clay at the bottom of the base (fig. 8d).

Building up the body

At the strongest point – the centre of the body where the armature is made fast to the horizontal arm – begin to lay on the clay,

---

Right **8 a** the figure iron; **b** the armature of the figure attached to the iron; **c** the hand armature; **d** the first layer of clay with the base.

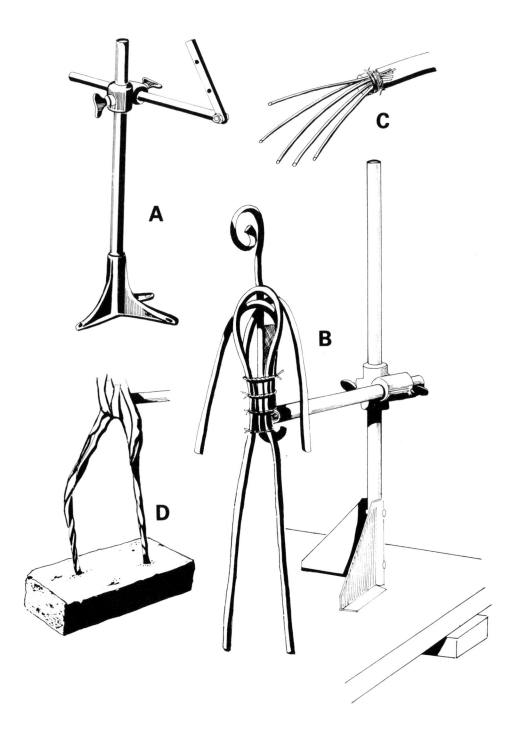

A

B

C

D

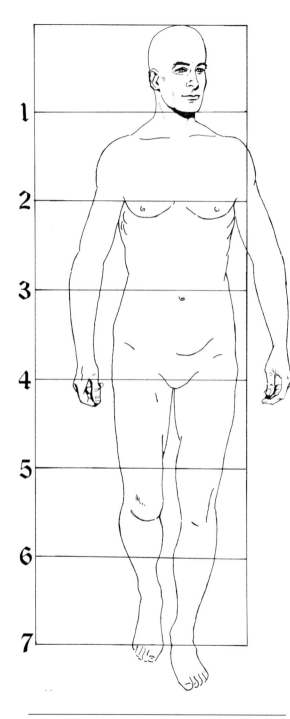

making sure that it penetrates the intersections of the armature and is held firmly. Work up and down from the centre, moving the leg, upper torso and head armature wires to the correct positions for your design. Watch the proportions carefully, but do not worry too much about thickness. It is better to keep the model on the thin side, because you can build up gradually to the required thickness in the right places later. Continue to work from the centre, progressing equally above and below. Surround the armature, except the arms for the moment, with clay. Modelling tools are of little help during this operation – your fingers are the most important tools for packing and forming the clay round the armature.

Having covered the whole of the armature with clay at this stage stand back and survey your handiwork. Your eyes will tell you whether the proportions are correct in relation to each other. Study carefully, because now is the time to correct these matters and make good, before you move on to modelling the details of the head and hands. Rotate your model and allow the light to strike it at various angles; this will show you where you have to build up and where you must smooth down. Now bend the arm wire armature back into its pre-arranged position and lay on the clay until the arms are at the same stage as the rest of your figure.

The head
The head is one part of the figure that is visible most of the time, so great care should be exercised in its modelling. These points are particularly important (see fig. 11):

1 the underside of the head where the features fit into the round section of the head

9 A guide to figure proportions.

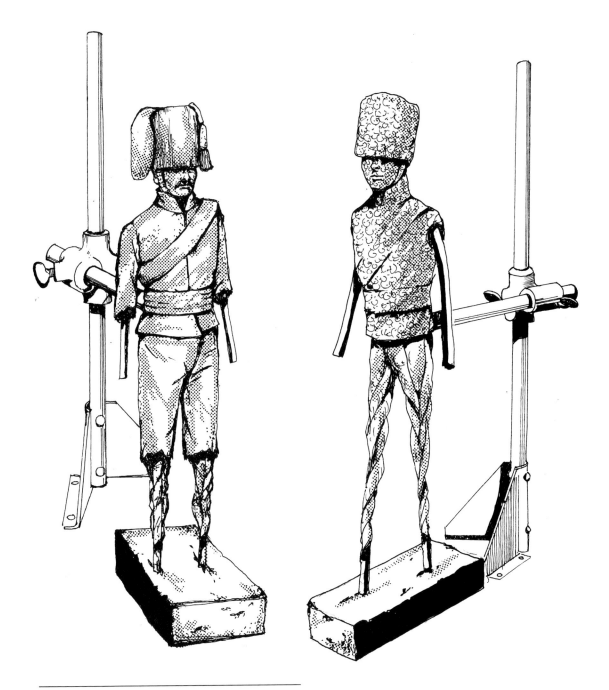

10 The half-finished armature, with the legs and arms left till last to allow the soft armature to be bent into position where necessary before being covered with clay.

2 the angle of the profile, from the chin to the top of the head

3 the nose, which starts just below the forehead *and* has a front and sides

4 the eyes, placed in the round part of the head to give a wide angle of vision

5 the mouth, semi-circular in shape

In general terms, the following proportions will help you model the head:

- the distances from the chin to the tip of the nose, from the nose to the brow and from the brow to the hairline are equal
- the distance from the centre of the mouth to the tip of the nose is the same distance as from the hairline to the top of the skull
- the ears are the same size as the distance from the tip of the nose to the browline
- the front edge of the ear is approximately half way between the front and back of the head
- the distance between the eyes is one eye length

The positioning of the head on the neck is very important. Place the round section of the head on a cylinder-shaped neck (fig. 11b) in line with the base of the ear. The neck is not a straight gradual line growing out from the body but rather a complete tube rising directly from the shoulders. Smooth down some clay to join the two pieces together. Now place this on a dowel stick and balance this in a bottle – this will give you more freedom for the delicate facial modelling.

With a wire-ended tool, mark a vertical centre line and then a horizontal line for the brows. With these basic lines, start building up the forehead. Now mark off with dividers the position of the ears, and place a large-headed pin in the clay at those points.

---

11 a the equal proportions of chin to nose, to brow to hairline. b the front edge of the ear is approximately half way between the front and back of the head.

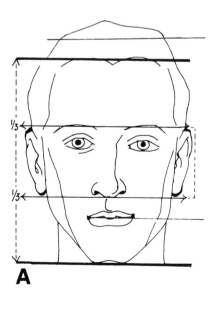

A

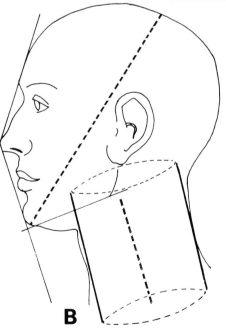

B

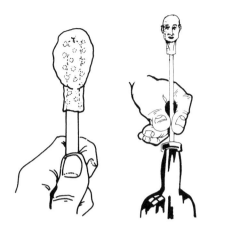

12 The head placed on a stick and balanced in a bottle.

You can then work out the length of the face in relation to the forehead, and place a pin at the point of the chin. Having satisfied yourself that this is correct, build up the cheekbones. Remember to keep the clay rounded over the forehead, under the chin and on the cheekbones.

Constantly check the head from all angles and especially from underneath. Do not proceed to the next stage until you feel that these proportions and positions are correct. The tendency to rush ahead hoping that the next operation will put things right is a fatal one – be patient!

Now form the jaw line, which starts from the points marked with pins indicating the

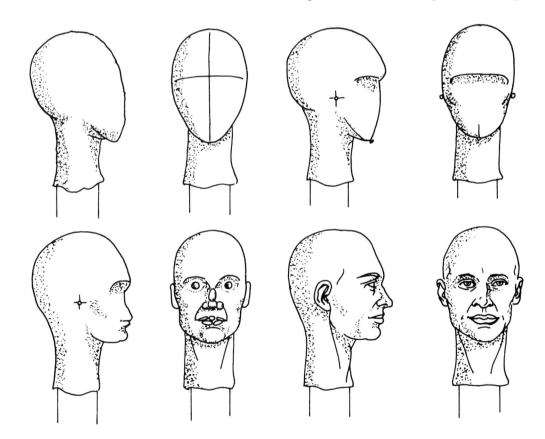

13 The stages in building up a head.

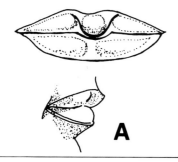

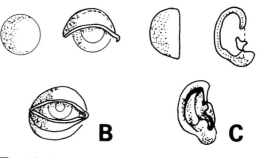

14 a a mouth; b an eye and lid; c an ear.

The hands

To model hands successfully you must study really carefully and copy either your own hand or that of a patient friend. Each finger must be modelled separately, starting with a small sausage shape and blending this into the mass of the back of the hand and palm (fig. 15). Notice the joints of the fingers and the protrusion of the knuckles, and show the fingernails clearly – these look very realistic when they are painted. Trace a few veins over the back of the hand. On the palm, follow as closely as you can the lines and formation of a real hand. When you are quite satisfied that a good job has been done and you have viewed your hands from every angle, then, and only then, smooth off.

ears and runs down to the point of the chin. This done, again remembering to round off the clay, you can form the mouth (fig. 14a). Watch the shape of the mouth carefully, taking note that the cheeks form the corners and that the supporting forms come up from the chin. The top lip should project further than the cheekbones.

With a small, round pellet of clay, form the eyeballs and place them in position. Over the eyeballs, and following their contours, add the eyelids; remember that the upper eyelid is heavier (fig. 14b).

Build on the nose, making sure that the bridge is formed just below the forehead, and finally, model the ears (fig. 14c). These must be viewed from all angles so that they are neither too flat nor too protruding. You can now take a last look at the head, and smooth down and tidy up as necessary.

The body

The rest of your figure will probably be concealed by clothes, either modelled on and painted or fashioned in materials, so

15 Building up a hand on top of thin wire extending from the arm.

Right 16 Building up a 54mm (2⅛in) figure using sections of clay (b).

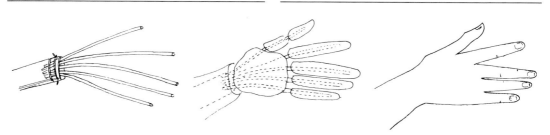

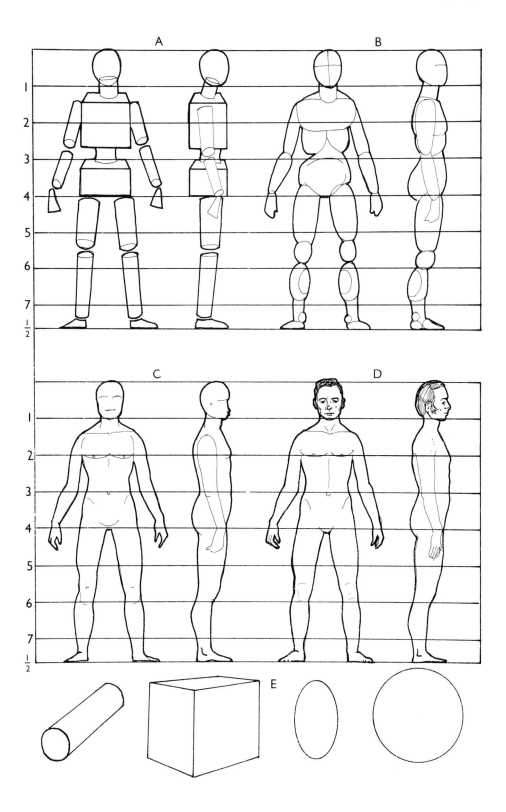

that it is not necessary to model in the muscles of the body with any great accuracy. However, just as a builder must know about the foundations and materials of his constructions, so must you have a basic knowledge of bones and muscles. Keen observation will show you how the muscles function within the framework of the bones, but a book on anatomy and a wooden 'lay figure' are well worth purchasing.

You are now ready to make a mould (see Chapter 4).

54mm (2⅛in) modelling (Plasticine)

The making of the simple basic figure for the 54mm (2⅛in) size model in Plasticine is very uncomplicated if the proportions in fig. 16 are followed. There is no armature whatsoever to build – your figure is modelled from several simple shapes.

Building the body

The basic shapes required are shown in fig. 16b. Use the cube shapes to form the main body, and build up the limbs using cylinders and circles, finishing with an egg-shape for the head. The egg-shape should measure about 8mm (⅝in) and with this unit of measurement, make the rest of the body conform. Although this is a basic shape the general proportions must still be correct; otherwise the later process will be an even greater problem. So work constantly with a pair of dividers, checking and rechecking all the time, and get the proportions right. Note how the legs support the pelvis block and the arms join the upper torso block. It may be helpful, once you have formed the basic figure shape, to use a knitting needle to

17 a the tools needed for 54mm (2⅛in) modelling: wire-ended tools, wooden spatulas and a pair of dividers; b rolling out Plasticine into simple shapes; c building up the figure using a knitting needle as the basic armature; d checking the measurements with dividers; e the finished head.

support the figure during the more specific modelling (fig. 17c).

Mark in the muscle formation, and gradually round off the forms. Follow the instructions on pp. 18–22 for the head. When the body is in this half-finished state, check all proportions with dividers – it would be very difficult to correct any mistakes after this. At this stage, it is best to keep the arms well away from the body and the legs running in parallel with the arms in the 'at ease' position.

It is not possible to model very fine detail on your Plasticine figure when working on such a small scale within an area of 8mm (⁵⁄₁₆in) for the features of the head or on a surface of approximately 6mm (³⁄₁₆in) for a well-defined hand, so the finer detail must be etched out when the basic model form is in another material, such as plaster (see pp. 32–33). Nonetheless, the main features must be clearly defined: the main folds of the uniform can be moulded in, and a clear indication of where the trousers end and the gaiters or boots begin, for example, can be shown.

When you have marked in all the necessary details on the main parts, including the extremities like hands and feet, carefully wash over with a brushful of paint thinner to smooth off all the hard edges. Your model is now ready for casting (Chapter 4).

Don't be discouraged if your first figures are not as successful as you would wish them to be. Simply roll the Plasticine back into a lump and start again.

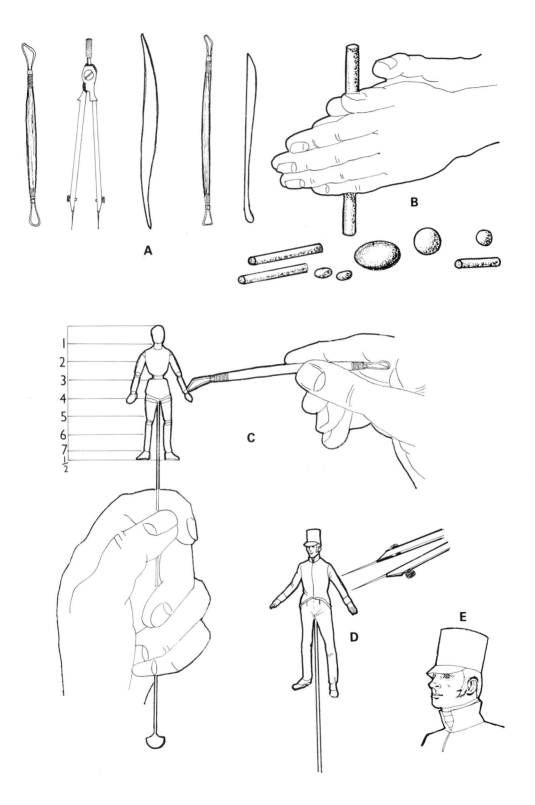

A

B

C

D

E

4 Moulds

Vinamold hot melt compound moulds

Your finished model should now be securely fastened to a base which can be made from clay, metal or a marble strip. Erect retaining walls (fig. 18): either an oiled strip of paper or a sheet of thin metal formed into a cylindrical shape and secured with string is easiest. The string is to ensure that the material does not unroll during the pouring of the hot compound. With the retaining wall or container erected, press clay or

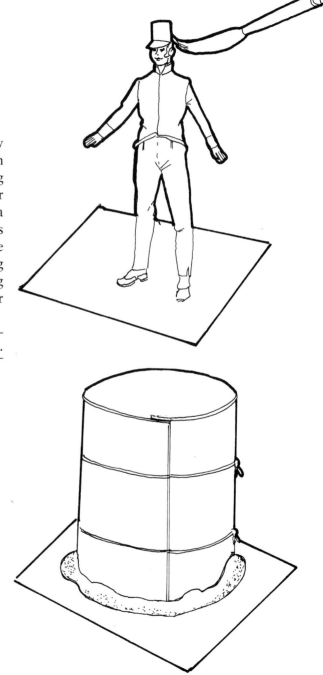

18 Building a wall around the Plasticine model.

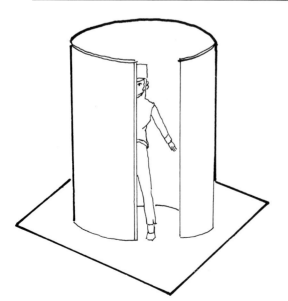

Plasticine around the bottom of the cylindrical shape to prevent the compound from seeping and leaking underneath.

Preparing the Vinamold

For the small quantities required, an aluminium or stainless steel saucepan can be used as a melting pot. A source of heat readily available to the average model maker is of course the ordinary household electric or domestic gas cooker with a diffusion mat placed over the hot plate or naked gas flame. Cut the Vinamold into very small pieces and place a handful into the saucepan on a moderate heat. It is important to stir the compound frequently until all the pieces have melted; when this has happened add

19 a pouring in the melted Vinamold;
b removing the wall when the Vinamould is set solid.

more pieces of Vinamold until you have as much as you need.

With the Vinamold in a completely liquid form, remove the saucepan from the source of heat and allow the liquid to cool to around 120°C (248°F) (the manufacturer's instructions should be read and carefully carried out). Pour the compound as quickly as possible in one pouring without stopping, as an even stream into the walls (fig. 19a). Bear in mind that at no time must the hot liquid be poured directly on to the model itself but between the model and the retaining wall, or better still against the side of the wall. As the mixture rises from the bottom upwards it forces the air from the finer detail of the model.

Leave the model to cool for several hours. To remove your model from the now flexible mould form it will be necessary to cut into the mould especially where there are deep undercuts (fig. 19b). To contain

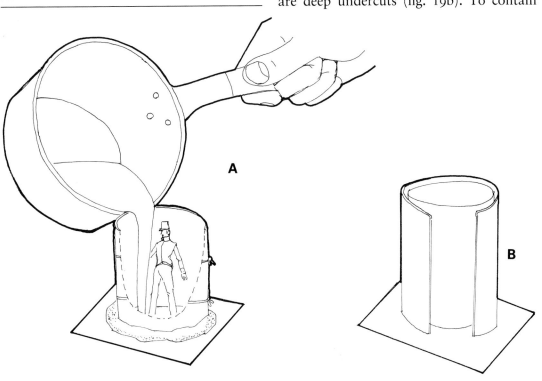

this flexible mould form a two-piece plaster case must be made.

Making the plaster case

Mark with a felt tip pen a line lengthwise around the mould, giving the half-way mark for the plaster mould. Make certain that the line marked runs down the sides of the figure and not down the front and back, using the feet holes as your guideline, otherwise the seal line from the casting will spoil the features of the face and other details on both front and back of the model.

Roughen up the surface of the rubber wall by making indentations into the mould so that the plaster will have sufficient keys to retain the rubber mould in position. Surround the rubber mould with a Plasticine strip along the ink mark and build a retaining wall around (fig. 20). Scoop retaining keys out of the Plasticine bed, one near each corner. Make some plaster into a

Right **21** **a** pouring in the plaster of Paris between the wall and mould; **b** removing the solid plaster support and cutting out keys; **c** repeating the process to complete the plaster support; **d** the Vinamold mould surrounded by the plaster mould and tied together to check that they fit.

creamy consistency and pour it over the mould to a height of not less than 25mm (1in) and if necessary make up a further bowl of plaster to fill the area to the same height (fig. 21a). As soon as the plaster is dry, reverse the mould and remove the Plasticine strip and wall. Brush the plaster surface with either soapy water or detergent and allow to dry. Build another retaining wall (fig. 21c) and repeat the process over again, then set aside to dry.

Remove the dry plaster cast from around the rubber mould. Place the mould on a bench and with a sharp knife cut open the mould along the centre parting line, which is marked in ink (fig. 22a). The ink mark has now served two purposes: that of dividing the plaster and that of showing the cut-line

20 Building a protecting wall for the plaster of Paris support.

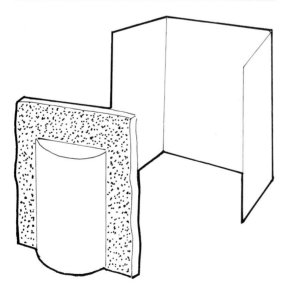

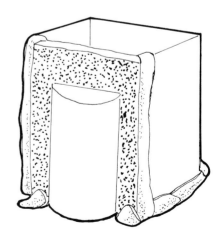

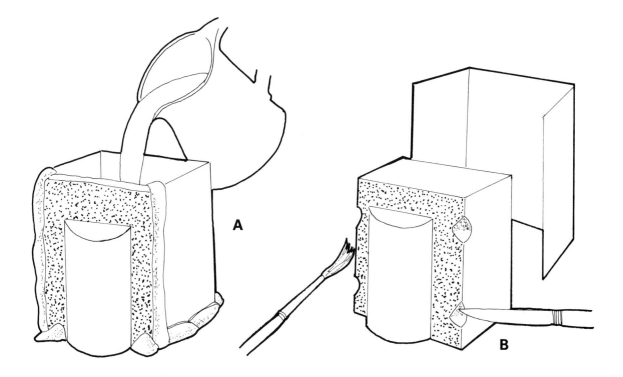

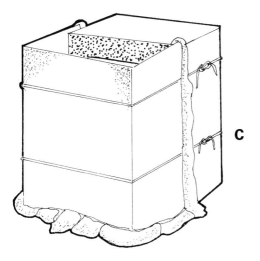

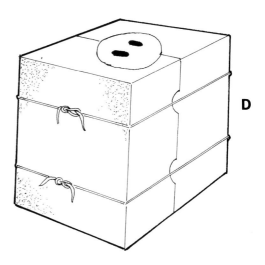

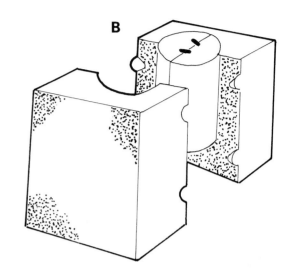

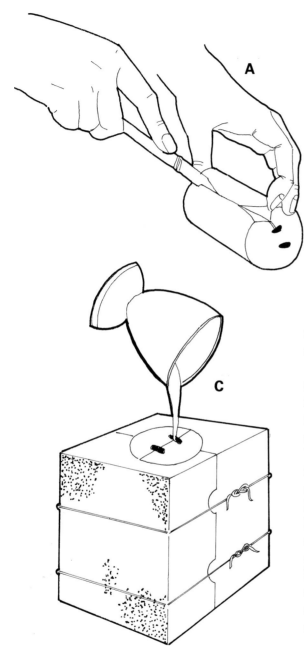

22 a cutting the Vinamold open along the marked line; b placing the cut Vinamold mould inside the plaster support; c pouring the plaster of Paris through the pour-holes.

for the extraction of the model and the subsequent castings.

Before removing the figure, cut a conical shape out of the mould up to the base of the feet. This shape must not be wider than the outside edges of the feet as this now constitutes the pour-hole. Cut open the Vinamold mould and very carefully remove the figure. Clean the mould carefully to ensure that there is no trace of clay or Plasticine left even in the tiny crease marks. Put the Vinamold mould back into one half of the plaster casing, and scrape out a conical shape continuing from the pour-holes. Repeat this process on the other half of the plaster casing so that you have a continuous pour-hole through both sections of the mould.

Making the model

You are now ready to proceed to the next operation, that of reproducing your original Plasticine or clay basic model into a more permanent substance. A plaster of Paris reproduction is ideal to make a detailed figure. To do this you will need: 1 cup of plaster of Paris; 1 cup of water; 1 small mixing bowl; 1 wooden mixing spoon; plaster hardener. Bind the mould, complete with outer plaster case, with string or strong elastic bands, and turn it over with the pour-holes uppermost, and make the mould secure on the table (fig. 22b).

Pour half the contents of the water into the mixing bowl. The amount of plaster hardener (if required) must be taken from the manufacturer's instructions. Now take the cup of plaster of Paris and with a to-and-fro movement over the mixing bowl sprinkle the plaster into the water. Continue to do this until the plaster is just below the surface of the water. Stir with the wooden mixing spoon until the mixture is a nice creamy consistency and then pour it steadily into the mould, allowing it to run in against the side or wall of the mould (fig. 22c).

After a waiting time of about half an hour the mould can be untied and the outer plaster case removed. Gently ease the flex-ible mould open and extract the reproduced basic figure of plaster.

Study the model very carefully for any air bubbles or blemishes.

Having checked that no faults exist, clean off any 'flash' which may have attached itself to the model with a fine file and very fine sandpaper, although this is rarely necessary.

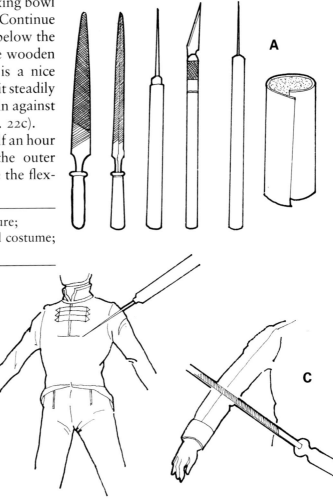

23 a tools for refining the plaster figure;
b and c adding detail to the face and costume;
d filing down flash lines.

Refining the model

With all the relative information to hand of the type of model soldier required, including any rough drawings of uniform and dress equipment that may be used, you can now develop the model.

Most students shy away from what seems quite a difficult procedure, although it is with practice a far quicker method for applying detail than any other I know. Here you need the techniques of an engraver with the aid of the metal and the simple wire-ended spatulas.

Gently scratch away at the surface of the plaster with the metal tools, marking out the folds, creases, seam lines, openings and

24 Opening a mould.

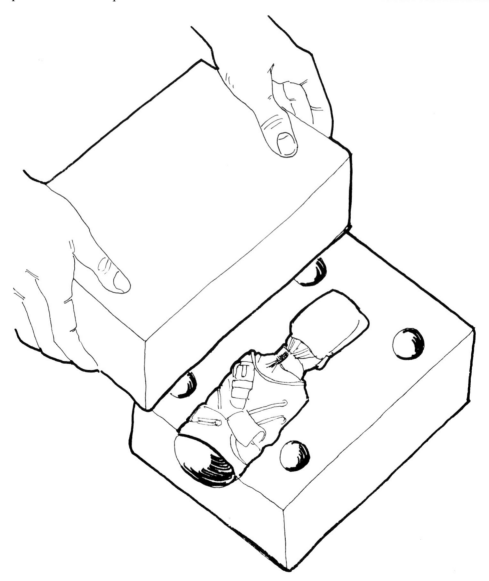

slashings, etc., of the tunics and breeches. The face can now receive more attention, so make the features sharper and more defined. The hands can also come in for the same treatment, especially the fingers.

Now to the fine detail of the uniform. Small pin-heads make excellent buttons; these can be cut and glued into their respective positions. Sheets of tin or lead foil can be utilised for many purposes, e.g. waist sashes, crossbelts, cartouches, cloaks, carry-straps, blanket rolls, shakos, cap peaks, saddle cloths, epaulettes, etc. Fine wire can be used to make plumes, feathers, fringes for the epaulettes, cords and tassels, etc. Small blocks of wood can be cut and made into packs. All these detail pieces can be fixed to the basic model with epoxy-resin adhesive.

I recommend that all weapons like swords, rifles and bayonets, unless the latter are made close in to the body, should be made in separate moulds because these would be rather difficult to extract from the rubber mould.

Cold-curing rubber mould making

Having added all the detail to your model you are now ready for the next stage: making the rubber mould. Because of its heat resistence and negligible shrinkage cold-curing silicone rubber is ideal for the model soldier enthusiast in preparing moulds for the making of metal and plastic type models. This room-temperature-curing silicone rubber can be purchased at most good art shops.

As plaster is porous, your model must be sealed, although this is not strictly necessary with cold-curing compounds. During cold weather, however, it is advisable to warm your model slightly, as cold air in the model on becoming warm will expand and cause bubbles when contact with the compound is made. A thin coat of a good liquid detergent brushed over the completed model and allowed to dry thoroughly will be sufficient to act as a seal.

The simplest mould is a one-piece mould. To make this, place the model on a bed of Plasticine, the bed being the depth of the vents or pouring channels attached to the model's feet. The Plasticine base will anchor the model down and prevent it from rising and floating away when the liquid rubber silicone is poured in. Now build the retaining wall in much the same way as for the Vinamold model (see p. 26), forming a sheet of thin metal into a cylindrical shape then securing with string or a piece of wire wound round and twisted at the ends with a pair of pliers (fig. 25a). The bottom of the retaining wall can be attached to the base by using rolls of Plasticine pressed firmly round; this secures the wall and prevents the fluid rubber from flowing from underneath.

Preparing the rubber

The rubber compound is mixed with a catalyst, which is supplied along with the compound. This will accelerate or retard the curing time, according to the manufacturer's instructions, which must be followed very carefully. They are easy to use and will faithfully reproduce your model down to the finest detail.

Following the manufacturer's instructions, mix the catalyst thoroughly into the silicone rubber by hand-stirring. During the mixing take great care to avoid trapping excessive air. The normal time for the rubber to reach the handling stage is roughly ten minutes, but this time depends on both the amount of catalyst used and the room temperature. Humidity and temperature play a decisive part in the drying time:

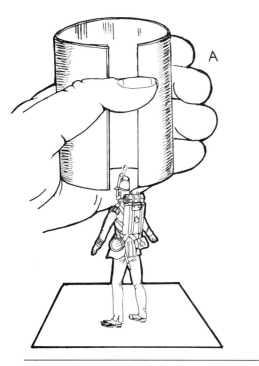

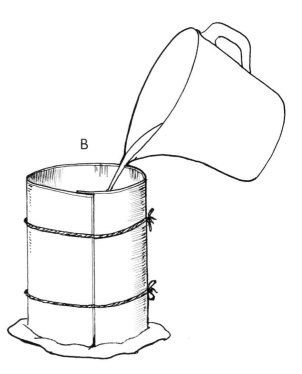

25 a building a retaining wall around the plaster figure; b pouring in the molten rubber.

low temperature and humidity will slow down the curing time whilst high temperature and humidity will speed up the curing time. Remember that the rubber will start to cure as soon as the catalyst has been dispersed in the rubber compound.

Pouring

When the rubber compound is ready to be handled, the job of pouring begins. Pour the rubber around the figure, making sure the flow of the pouring is either down the side of the retaining wall or between the model and the wall but never directly over the model itself (fig. 25b). Try to pour the rubber all at once and in a steady stream. If there are deep undercuts on your model, you may need to brush some of the compound mixture onto these parts immediately before pouring; this will help to eliminate unwanted air bubbles.

Continue pouring until 13mm (½in) above the top of the figure. After making certain that the base holding the liquid mould is standing level, leave the mould to cure for 48 hours.

When the rubber mould has cured, remove the cylindrical retaining wall of metal. Your master model figure is now completely enclosed in a solid cylinder of rubber. The next stage is to make a plaster casing mould, following the instructions on pages 28–30. When this is completed, remove the figure from the rubber mould, and put it somewhere very safe for future use. After the pour-holes are cut out, dust the inside of the rubber mould with graphite powder. This

Right 26 a building a retaining wall in Plasticine and hollowing out keys; b pouring the plaster over the horizontal model (not directly on to the figure); c removing the Plasticine retaining wall, and the resulting side view (d); e placing the two halves of the plaster mould together ready for pouring.

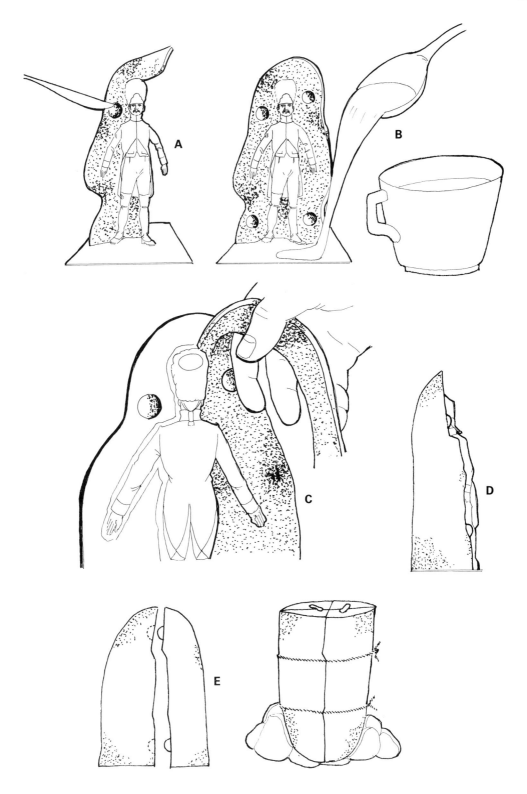

will ensure a good casting. Now secure the rubber mould inside the plaster casing, and you are ready to cast your first figure.

Plaster mould making

Plaster is an alternative and cheaper material to rubber from which to make your mould. There are two alternative methods, described below, both of which have advantages and disadvantages – choose whichever suits your purpose best. Generally, however, plaster does have certain drawbacks as a mould material. First, there is the vulnerability of the mould itself. Being plaster and not very thick, it can easily be broken if not handled with great care. Secondly, the excessive heat of the molten metal destroys detail very quickly, lifting the surface off the plaster. I recommend the use of plaster moulds only if

a *the amount of castings are few in number and no great detail is required, and*
b *a basic figure is required that will be cleaned up, have greater detail added and then recast in a rubber mould.*

Method 1

Map out the model into two sections by placing strips of Plasticine or metal around the figure to form a fence or boundary, and scoop holes out of this wall to act as keys (fig. 26a). Once this is completed, mix enough plaster of Paris to commence work on the mould. If you are making a 54mm (2⅛in) model the plaster should be spooned over rather than poured on. When sufficient thickness of plaster has been laid on, leave aside to dry.

When dry, remove the boundary strips and make any slight damage to the model good. Lightly wash over the surface of the half-mould with soapy water or liquid detergent. Repeat the procedure for the other half of the mould. When the second half of the mould is dry, gently ease the mould apart and remove the Plasticine model. Thoroughly clean the mould to remove any trace of Plasticine from the tiny crevices with a wire-ended tool in order not to damage the detail that is so necessary on such a small model. Then leave the mould to dry out completely for 24 hours.

Warning: When completely dry, it is essential that there is no mixture whatsoever left in the plaster mould when the molten metal is poured in. This could be the cause of a 'blow back', which could result in an injury. Always ensure that the plaster mould is absolutely dry before commencing to pour in the hot metal.

Method 2

Apply three coats of shellac to your Plasticine figure, allowing each coat to dry before brushing on the next. When the figure is thoroughly dry, this will form a hard outer covering to prevent damage when pressing it gently but firmly into the clay bed. Mark a dividing line around the side of the figure with felt-tip pen; this will be the predetermined half-way parting line for your two-piece mould. Do this very carefully to ensure easy parting.

Prepare a bed of clay 25mm (1in) thick and press the figure firmly in up to the dividing ink mark. Smooth the clay down tight up to the half-submerged figure, allowing for the feet to be the pour-holes. Scoop out a conical depression mark in the clay about 25mm (1in) above the head of the figure by using the paddle end of the metal modelling spatula. Repeat this on

27 A British Artillery Officer of 1917, wearing a soft topped cap (the wire being removed), the 'British Warms', which carried the badge of rank on the shoulder straps, Bedford cord breeches, boots and gaiters. *Latex composition, 30cm (12in) high*

28 Field Marshall Rommel. *Latex composition,*
30cm (12in) high

either side of the figure about 25mm (1in) away. These are the keys for the mould alignment.

Brush the half-protruding figure with a coat of oil to prevent it adhering to the plaster. The bed of clay may be left untouched as it has its own resistance to the plaster. Surround the figure with a wall of either wood or Plasticine; if wood is used, brush with a light coating of oil to prevent the plaster sticking. Mix the plaster of Paris as before (p. 31) to a fine creamy substance, then with the aid of a cup pour the liquid plaster around the edges of the wall allowing the plaster to flow towards the figure. This must be a firm steady flow with no splashing, and on no account must you pour directly onto the figure. When the covering of the figure is complete, bring the plaster to a thickness of about 25mm (1in). Leave the half-completed model aside and allow to dry.

When dry, turn the mould over and remove the bed of clay, which is now uppermost, revealing the back of the model figure now embedded in the plaster. Now wash over the plaster with soapy water or liquid detergent and lightly coat the back of the protruding figure with oil. Repeat the process of preparing the plaster and covering the rest of the model. Leave to dry.

When completely dry, ease the mould apart very gently and carefully. With the separation of the two halves and the figure removed, the mould is now ready for making the cast figures.

5 Casting

Metal

A good quality metal ladle is the only piece of equipment the amateur model maker need buy for casting. The choice of metal or combination of alloys for the model is really

29 A finished metal 54mm (2⅛in) figure, smaller than the original model. Note that the hands and baton are cast separately.

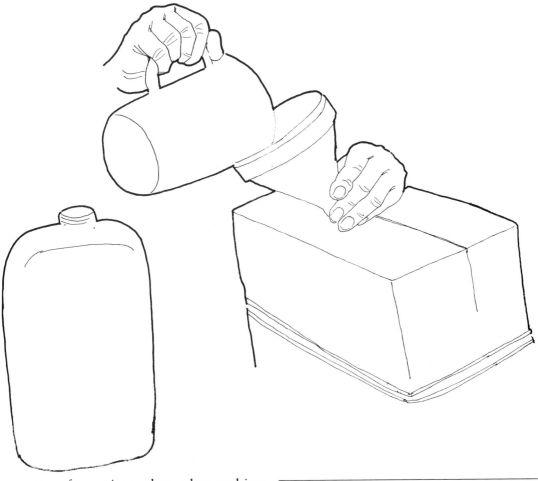

a matter of experience, but a low-melting alloy is easier to handle and better for animation.

The mould must be securely bound and placed on a bench or table before you start preparing the metal. Place sufficient low-melting alloy in the ladle and take it to a heat source. Either gas or electricity can be used, whichever is more readily available. The correct time to start pouring is when the silvery surface of the metal begins to turn blue or brownish in colour. The best method is by pouring gradually and carefully, allowing only a few drops at a time to enter the mould. After the mould has been filled, wait a few minutes to allow the

30 Latex poured into a securely-tied mould through a funnel.

metal to solidify. If the mould is plaster, remove the model quickly, as extended heat within the mould can be damaging to the impression.

Latex

This is an alternative material for making models from plaster moulds.

Reassemble the parts of the plaster mould, ensuring that the registration keys fit exactly into each other. Secure the mould tightly with string or elastic bands. If it does not bind tight enough, you can fit small pieces of wedge-shaped wood between the string and the wall of the mould, thus pulling the string taut.

The composition comes from the manufacturer in liquid latex and filler paste form; by varying the proportions of the filler paste to the liquid latex, the degree of hardness or flexibility of the finished model can be controlled. Thoroughly mix the two contents into a smooth paste and allow to stand for about 24 hours to dispel air bubbles. Slightly dampen the mould before pouring the mixture in. To minimize flash pour a very small amount of the latex composition into the mould and allow it to run along the seam or joining line, then empty this out and return it to the container. To lessen the possibility of air bubbles being trapped in the mould, balance it at an angle of 45 degrees – a wedge-shaped piece of wood cut at this angle on which the mould can rest is very useful.

Completely fill the mould with the composition at a steady flow, giving a gentle tap to the mould during this operation to assist the liquid in reaching the small and more detailed cavities. The level of the com-

31 An Indian soldier ('Skinner's Horse') modelled in eight parts.

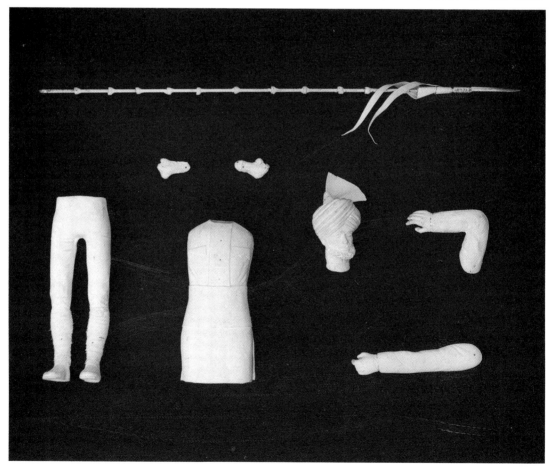

position will drop due to the absorption of the moisture from the compound by the porous plaster mould, so you will need to top it up constantly during the build-up period. Although the time taken for this build-up varies according to the shape and formation of the mould, a rough guide is about 15 to 20 minutes.

After this time, invert the mould and pour the residue of the compound carefully back into the container for further use. You can then place the plaster mould containing the deposited rubber skin of the gelled latex composition on the plaster mould surface either in a warm atmosphere and allow to dry out for a few hours, or in an oven with a temperature of between 50° and 70°C (120° and 158°F), which will make it dry out (vulcanize) in about 30 minutes. Drying time is again governed by both the shape and size of the mould and the filler loading. When dry, carefully untie the mould, ease gently apart and dismantle.

After the casting has been removed from the mould place it in a safe place and allow to dry (mature) at normal room tempera-ture. When completely dry, there will be a shrinkage of about 10 per cent. The flash line, owing to the liquid composition seeping into the seam lines of the mould, can be removed with sandpaper or a small in-expensive buffing motor.

Making a mould in several parts

Although a two-piece mould is in some ways the easier method, it is quite possible, and often helpful, to make a latex figure in parts, casting each part of the body separately and joining the pieces together in much the same way as model soldier kits (see Chapter 2). In addition to the materials mentioned in that chapter, you will need a tube of rubber-based adhesive and some fine sandpaper sheets.

32 A selection of plaster heads modelled and cast separately to fit a standard 30cm (12in) body.

Method

Examine the latex parts for traces of flash and remove any with a sharp knife. Smooth over the seam lines with fine sandpaper.

The legs: these may be cast separately or as a pair. If cast separately, they should be joined together and attached to a wooden base with epoxy-resin adhesive, which not only sticks the parts together permanently but also acts as a filler and conceals the butted joints. Choose the stance for the feet and mark this on the base. Smear the bottom of the feet and the marked positions on the base with the adhesive and press the two firmly together. Set aside to dry for about 24 hours.

33 The back and front of a plaster head mould. Note that the neck extension acts as the pour-hole as well as fitting into the body.

Right **34** A Punjab Musalman of the 30th Punjabis wearing the popular long khaki shirt, or kurta, worn over the plus-four loose trousers. The Kurta had pockets and shoulder straps with the British-type military badges and buttons. He is also wearing the bandolier, brown leather waist belt, khaki coloured puttees and boots, and is carrying a Lee Enfield rifle. *Latex composition, 30cm (12in) high*

The head: the neck becomes the pour hole for the head, and this pour hole should be just large enough to fit into the neck opening of the main body tightly. Before pressing the head down, lightly smear around the edge of the neck hole and the neck of the head with the rubber-based adhesive, then press down, manoeuvring the head into the required position. By using the rubber adhesive you can alter the position without much trouble or damage to the model.

The arms: join the hand castings to the arms, again using rubber-based adhesive. Now attach the arms to the body at the shoulder joints, again using the pour hole extensions as the connection point, and temporarily glue them down.

Take a long hard look at the figure, check its attitude and make any adjustment neces- sary. When you are satisfied with the figure, fill in all the joins at the neck, wrist and shoulders with epoxy resin and smooth down with a slightly wet toothpick. When this is finished, stand the body aside for about 24 hours to dry.

For the final assembly, smear the outside of the waistband at the top of the legs and the inside of the waistband attached to the trunk with epoxy-resin adhesive and bring the two parts gently together, again ensuring a tight fit. Twist and turn into the right attitude, and press firmly down. Place the figure in a safe place to dry off.

When the figure is dry, check all the joins. Any excess adhesive that may have been forced out of the joins should now be cleaned off with a sharp knife and sandpapered.

6 Equipment

Material	Use
nylon hair, various colours	horse's mane and tail, wigs
patches of leather, dyed or painted as required	waist belts, cross belts, pouches, backpacks, pistol holsters, horse harness, general horse furniture (saddles, bridles, etc)
felt material in various colours	horse cloths and shabraques; particularly useful because doesn't leave unsightly thread ends
large-headed pins	realistic buttons; beaten flat as knives and short bayonets
metal sheets (pliable)	breast-plates, scabbards, helmet-plates, badges, decorations for horse harness, man and horse armour, sword hilts, flags and pennants
thread, various colours and thicknesses	body lines, aiguillettes, cap lines, barrel belts, flounders and tassels, fringes, plumes, etc.
wire, various gauges	wide variety of uses, including horse harnesses, walking sticks and umbrellas
strips of tempered steel	sword blades: shape and sharpen in a vice, wrap round with softer sheet metal
metal tubing, small diameter	rifle barrel, sword scabbard (when flattened)
fine chain	chain and pickers on cross belts, whistle chain on pockets, protection chain on certain helmets, chin chains and horse chains
nylon fur	bearskin crests
braids	decoration and edging

The following is a list of tools required to make fairly simple equipment for metal and latex model soldiers:

- small table grip-type vice
- set of small drills with handle
- pair of wire cutters
- block of metal and a hammer
- pair of small sharp-ended scissors
- pair of long-nosed pliers

Some of the larger pieces of equipment, such as helmets and cannons, will need to be cast in metal separately – the procedure for this is exactly the same as for the figures. Smaller items, however, that distinguish particular soldiers and add important touches of authenticity, can be made very simply using odd bits of wire, rope, cotton, etc. Below is a list of the typical materials and what they can be used to make. The list is not exhaustive, and you can use your imagination to adapt any odd scraps into suitable equipment for your soldiers.

35 Back view of a young drummer boy of the 77th Middlesex Regiment of the 1812 Peninsular War period. He is wearing the reverse colours of the regiment and the 'stovepipe' shako, which was worn by the British Infantry since 1800. *Latex composition, 30cm (12in) high*

36 A British Grenadier of 1751, wearing the Grenadier hat with a galloping white horse of Hanover embroidered on the turned up front with the words '*nec aspera terrent*' ('difficulties be damned').

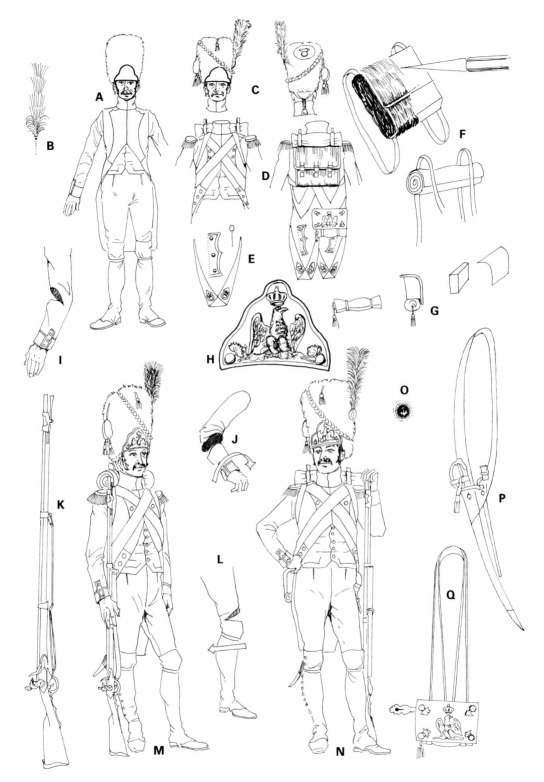

A French Infantry soldier *(fig. 37)*

The basic figure for this can be in either metal or latex. The figure has already had the jacket and trouser markings engraved on. The plume and tassels for the hat (c) and the epaulettes are made from fine fuse wire twisted together. Pins are stuck into the jacket front to make buttons, and thin strips of metal or plastic sheeting are bent round and attached to the figure to form cross belts (d). The turnbacks on the coat are formed from metal or plastic sheeting in a similar way and attached with pins that form extra buttons (d and e). The back pack (f) is made from a small block of balsa wood and inscribed with a knife to give a furred look. A thin roll of metal or plastic cut to size then fits into the blanket holder. The cartridge box is made from a smaller block shape of balsa wood with a front cover of metal or plastic. The cover, which has the Imperial Eagle and grenades adhered to it, should be cut a little larger than the wood in order to give an overlap (g). The forage cap or 'Bonnet de Police' is a piece of rolled metal or plastic fitted with a fine wire tassel, then glued to the underside of the balsa wood. The front cover is then placed over the wood and glued down (q). The hat plate should be cut to the same shape as h and engraved with the Imperial Eagle as for the cartridge box cover. This is then glued to the centre of the cap. The rifle is cast separately, following the same procedure as making a model figure.

The arms and legs can now be animated (i, j and l).

Left **37** A French Infantry soldier: **a** finished engraved model; **b** plume; **c** front and back of hat plus grenade; **d** front and back of coat; **e** pocket and turnbacks on coat; **f** back pack; **g** cartridge box; **h** hat plate; **i, j** and **l** animation of model; **k** the rifle; **m** and **n** different animated figures; **o** tri-coloured cockade; **p** hanger sword; **q** Imperial Guard's cartridge box.

A British Infantry soldier *(fig. 38)*

Buttons and cross belts are added in the same way as above (**a–c**). The epaulettes, again made from fine wire, are attached with a pin that then acts as a button (**f** and **k**). The water bottle is made from a circular piece of balsa engraved with lines, and a thin piece of metal is then attached to form the carrying strap (**e**). The shako is decorated with a false front of metal, again engraved with the regimental emblem, and draped with a tassel (**h**). The back pack is made from balsa wood and a metal roll (see p. 51) plus a semi-circular piece of balsa with thin strips of metal attached as if threaded through (**q**). The bayonet is made from a beaten-out pin with the head bent over and attached to a small funnel of metal (**p**). This is then attached to the 'Brown Bess' rifle, cast separately (**l**). The side pack or bread bag (**n**) is made from metal, making sure to make it look suitably full and saggy.

Right **38** A British Infantry soldier: **a** engraved figure ready for buttons; **b** cross-belt with cross belt plate; **c** back view with cross belt; **d** shako with false front, hat plate and plume; **e** water bottle; **f** and **k** epaulette and button; **g** and **i** finished model; **h** shako cords; **j** cross-belt with buckled ends, cartridge pouch and regimental device; **l** 'Brown Bess' rifle; **m** bayonet scabbard; **n** bread bag or side pack; **o** shoulder straps plus chest strap; **p** bayonet; **q** back-pack equipment; **r** backview with shoulder strap arrangement.

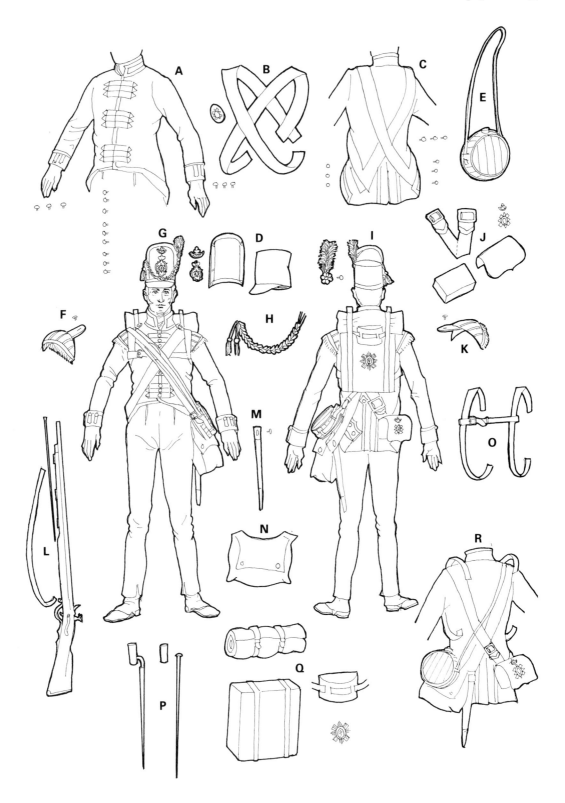

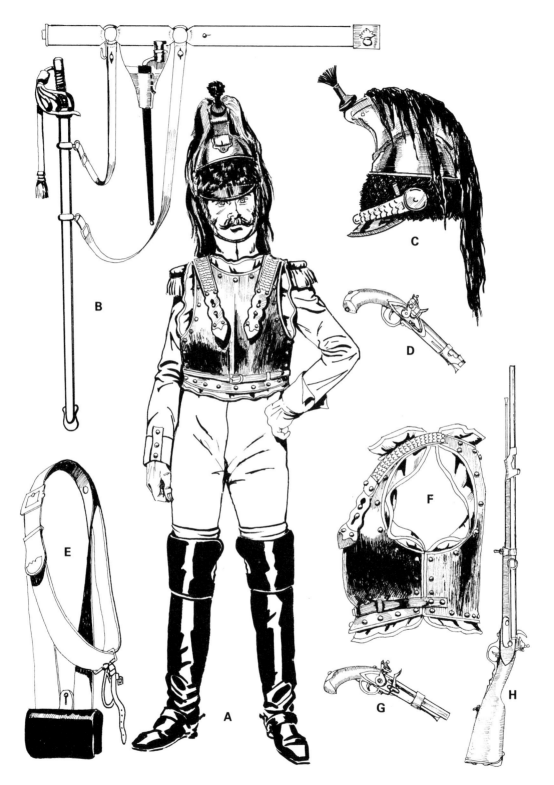

A French Cuirassier (fig. 39)

The complicated sword and bayonet fixture here (**b**) is made in a similar way to that described above, using metal strips for the sword and belt, a beaten-out pin for the bayonet, thin wire for the sword tassel. The helmet is modelled and cast separately. The headband is then roughed up with metal-ended tools, and fuse wire is stuck on and cut unevenly to create the plume (**c**). The breast plate, which makes this soldier so distinctive, is made from sheets of thin metal cut to shape and then bent and moulded to fit the figure (**f**). This is then attached with pins to complete the article (**a**). The guns and pistols are cast separately.

Left **39** A French Cuirassier, c.1812:
a complete figure; **b** sword belt, sword knot, slings and bayonet frog plus steel sabre;
c helmet; **d** cavalry-type pistol mark AN IX;
e the pouch and carbine belt; **f** two-piece steel cuirass; **g** cavalry pistol mark AN XIII; **h** carbine musket mark AN IX.

A soldier of the 2nd Lancers of the Imperial Guard (fig. 40)

The main item here is the hat (**b**), which can be either modelled as part of the figure and then be decorated with a plume, hat plate and tassels later, or cast separately. The cockade (**d**) is made from fuse wire. The jacket is decorated as usual with pins for buttons and fuse wire for tassels and epaulettes (**c** and **e**).

Right **40** A 2nd Lancer of the Imperial Guard: **a** the complete lancer; **b** a chapka, minus plume; **c** front view of kurta; **d** tri-colour cockade; **e** epaulette with fringe; **f** back view of kurta; **g** side view of chapka with tassels and head cords plus plume.

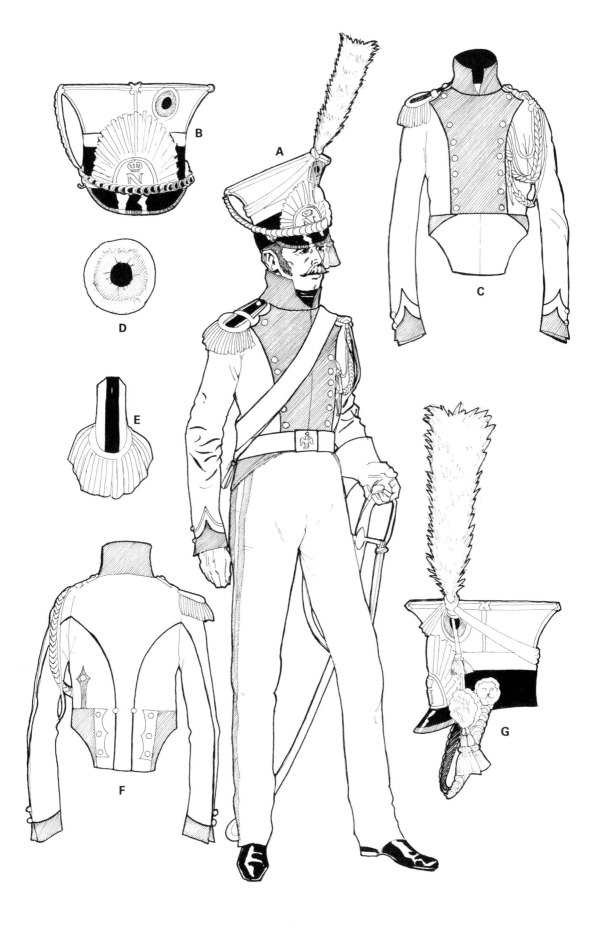

A

B

C

D

E

F

G

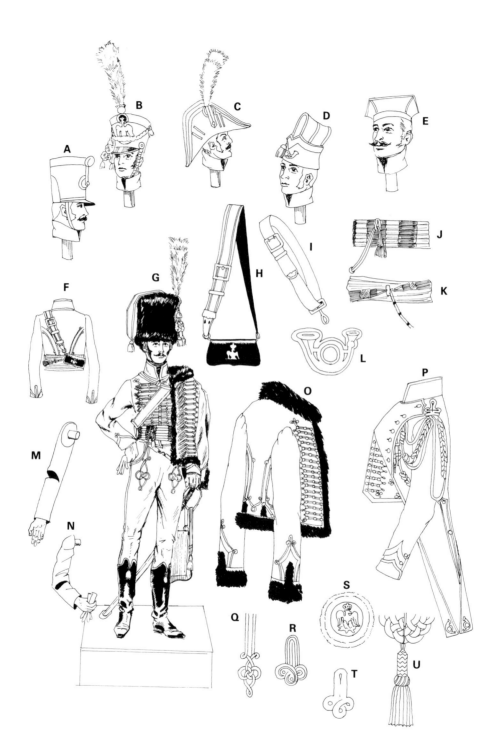

A Chasseur à cheval of the Guards, 2nd regiment *(fig. 41)*

A selection of heads and headdresses (**a–e**) that have here been modelled separately from the body. They could each fit the same body and would suit different ranks or situations. The fine frogging and tassels that decorate the pelisse (**o**) and the undress coat (**p**) are made from twisting fuse wire and sticking it in place with pins, which again form buttons. The fur trimming is made from thin metal sheeting with rasped edges and the main surface roughed up. The pouch bag (**h**) is made from a small piece of balsa wrapped round with thin metal sheeting and attached to another thin strip of metal to form the strap. For the posture shown here (**g**) the arms need to be converted after the figure is cast (**m** and **n**).

Left **41** Chasseur à cheval of the guard: **a** full dress shako, 1815; **b** Young Guard headdress; **c** a bicorne (1803–4) for walking-out dress; **d** Chasseur's Bonnet de Police, 1813; **e** Officer's undress hat of 2nd regiment; **f** back view of Chasseur's dolman; **g** full-dress uniform of service escort duty 1805–14; **h** pouch belt; **i** carbine cartouche; **j** and **k** barrel belt; **l** bugle-horn badge; **m** and **n** animation of arm; **o** back view of pelisse as seen when hanging from left shoulder; **p** undress coat; **q** Austrian knot for breeches; **r** shoulder strap; **s** cockade with eagle device on front; **t** shoulder strap; **u** flounders and tassel worn on colpack.

7 Horses

The clay model

Prepare a rough sketch for yourself as a guide (fig. 42). The scale of the drawing should be sufficiently accurate to give a true conception of the proportions of your horse. You can assess these by careful study of live models and photographs. Think first of whether you want your horse to be standing still, walking, rearing, grazing, trotting, etc., because it is important to get the centre of gravity in the right place. You should get this right at the sketching stage because otherwise it will cause you trouble later on.

The armature

To make a horse of 30cm (12in) high in latex composition, you should start by making an armature of 31cm (12½in) from the base to the top of the head. Your finished model will always turn out slightly smaller than your preliminary model.

42 Preparatory drawing showing the centre of gravity in a rearing horse.

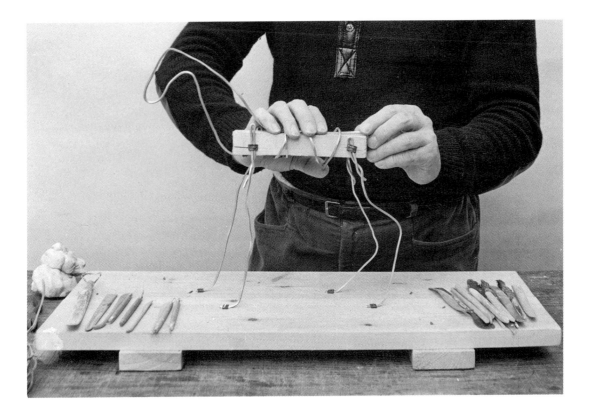

43 Building the armature for the horse with wood and wire.

Take a piece of wood 18cm × 2.5cm × 2.5cm (7in × 1in × 1in), which will act as the body of the model. Onto this fix the wire for the legs, neck and head (fig. 43). To form these, use 25mm (1in) diameter square aluminium wire. Cut four pieces of wire, approximately 30cm (12in) long. Bend the tops over about 2.5cm (1in), squeeze the ends together and then attach firmly with staples or nails to the extremities of the wooden piece. Cut a further length 60cm (24in) long for the head, allow some 10–12cm (4–5in) of wire to be stapled down the length of the wood, then staple down about 7.5cm (3in) of wire on the underside of the wood. Shape the neck and

head, keeping them in proportion to each other.

Bend over the leg armatures once again and fix them to a modelling board. Fix two transverse pieces of wood 7.5cm × 1.9cm (3in × ¾in) underneath the board to prevent it warping.

Take a rod of iron 20cm (8in) high and fix this to the wooden base (see fig. 44). Rest the wooden model on the iron upright, which is detached after the first half of the mould has been cast. Wrap some more wire around the wooden body piece, and the armature is complete.

The head and the legs must now be given the attitude and stance you have decided upon. Adjust the wire for the head, taking care to follow the line of the spinal column. Gently put the wire of the legs in place.

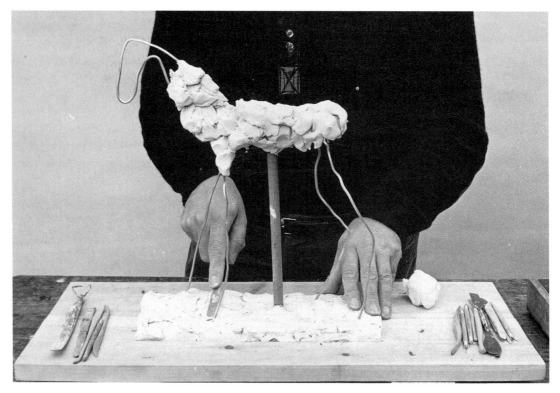

44 Laying the clay on the armature, making sure that the horse's hooves are embedded in the base so as to form pour-holes later.

Modelling

Once the armature is completed and you are satisfied with its shape and attitude, you can start to lay on the clay. First of all, lay some onto the base, about 1.8cm (¾in) thick. The ends of the leg armature will fit into this and when the base is cut away later the extra clay on the ends of the hooves will form the very important pour holes of the finished model, through which the latex is poured.

Now cover the whole of the armature with clay. Do this by adding a very little at a time until you reach the correct bulk of the horse. It is much easier to build up your figure than to have to take away a lot of excess material.

Once you have covered the armature completely by putting on small pieces of clay and smoothing them down, make a spine line down the back of the horse. This will become the guide for the construction of the body as seen from above. Next, mark the side view from just under the jaw of the horse's head, down the centre of the chest, between the forelegs and under the belly, giving the lower line of the body. Then move up between the hind legs to the crupper or tail piece to join up with the spinal line. This has established the lower and upper neck line, the chest and the stomach muscles.

Working from the top and from the buttocks towards the shoulder muscles, smooth in the round lines and muscles of your horse. Again working from the back, indicate the muscles on the back legs. Now, from the shoulders downwards, indicate the

45 Finishing off the modelling.

Below **46** The relative proportions of a horse.

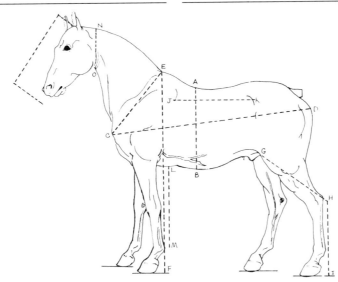

chest muscles. Smooth in the shape of the head and the legs from both sides. You will probably find it helpful to have a book on the anatomy and muscles of the horse open in front of you at this point.

If it is necessary to finalize the stance of your figure at this point; this can be accomplished by easing the wire gently within the clay. You now have a roughed-in model of the horse, with all the muscles indicated and in the desired position.

If you take the head of your horse as the unit of measurement, it should be an easy matter now to check the proportions (see fig. 46). Note that the head is made slightly smaller than is normal in a live horse. This is simply artistic licence, You will see that

your horse will take on an air of elegance and gracefulness that might be lacking if the head is too large and heavy. Here is a list of useful comparisons (see fig. 46):

1 *The size of the head should approximately equal the following:*
- from A (the back) to B (the belly)
- from E (the withers) to C (the point of the shoulder)
- from G (the stifle) to H (the hock)
- from H (the hock) to I (the bottom of the hoof)
- from J (the shoulder) to K (the hip)
- from L (the girth) to M (the fetlock)

2 *Half the size of the head is approximately equal to the distance from N (the crest) to O (the lower jaw)*

---

47 The finished clay model, still on the iron support.

Troopers of the Household cavalry. The Royal Horseguards (the blue uniforms) and the Life Guards (the red uniforms). They are depicted here on dismounted guard duty.

An incident in the Battle of Waterloo depicting a Polish Lancer of the Guard, 1st Regiment of Napoleon's Bodyguard and a British sergeant of the 3rd Foot Regiment and a French Dragoon.

3 *Two and three-quarters the size of the head is approximately equal to:*

- from E the withers to F the bottom of the foreleg hoof
- from C the point of the shoulder to D the point of the buttocks

These measurements should not present too much difficulty if you use a pair of callipers or dividers.

At this stage, stand back and survey your work. See that the final movement is correct and that the muscular heaviness is in the right position; check that all the anatomical indications are there and are united into one composition. In the smoothing off, the next operation, great care must be taken in the forming of the muscles. Make sure that there are no deep hollows and allow the muscles to meet in a gentle line. This will give an overall picture of muscles that are in a state of action and muscles that are in repose.

Finishing off

The finishing off is really a matter of choice and will depend on the purpose for which the model is required. Where a certain realism is essential, one must adhere to a deliberate smoothness and finish. The surface of the model must acquire a skin texture and a feathered effect, especially over the front of the chest and over the hindquarters. A study of a live model will show you these details precisely. If, how-

48 The model surrounded by a finished dividing band.

ever, you have made a model with clear, cleanly formed lines which reveal the full power and elegance of this magnificent beast, then it is quite unnecessary to smooth and finish off.

Making the mould

Once the clay model is completed, you can move on to the next step: that of making the mould, in this instance in plaster of Paris.

For this horse, I suggest you make a two-piece mould, although most models can be made from as many pieces as you find convenient.

Preparing the model

First of all, it is necessary to frame the horse in a band of clay on the predetermined line of division to separate the model into two parts.

Make a roll of clay, about 2.5cm (1in) thick and at least 30cm (12in) long. Put it on a board or a laminated kitchen table and beat it with the hand until it is absolutely flat and about 6mm (¼in) thick. Smooth it out with a small glass jar or bottle then cut it lengthways with a knife to a width of 4cm (1½in). This done, fix it along the top of the clay model so that the model is divided into a front and a back part. Start at the top of the head at the crest, work along the centre of the back towards the buttocks and down the middle of the back part of the left hind leg to the base. Make up further bands of clay. Then proceed to place the band up the middle of the front of the left hind leg, under the crutch, down the middle back of the right hind leg to the base; then work up the middle of the right hind leg, across the underside of the stomach to a point at the

top of the left foreleg, then down the middle of the foreleg to the base. Then go up the middle of the left foreleg, across the underside of the chest, down the middle back of the right foreleg to the base, and up the middle of the right foreleg, continuing up the centre of the neck, and down the centre of the jaw to the muzzle. Move the boundary up through the centre of the head, up the front of the left ear, across the nape of the neck, over the middle of the right ear and join up the band at the crest.

These bands must adhere to the surface of the clay model without pressing too heavily against it. The seal must fit tight, leaving no spaces between the band and the model, but must still be able to be removed easily. Now strengthen the bands from behind with small slips or supports of clay. Indent the clay surface of the band at regular intervals to make keys that will allow the second half of the mould to be fitted snugly and neatly to the first. This half becomes the *anterior* half of the mould.

Lay some soft, moistened paper over the back side of the model to prevent the liquid plaster, when thrown, from falling on the half of the model not being cast.

The hooves of the horse will be cast to form the pour-holes, formed from the 2.5cm (1in) clay base by scraping away the clay and forming inverted V shapes from the hooves down to the wooden base (see p. 62). They should splay out at the base to about 2.5cm (1in) in diameter, ensuring a good vent for the liquid latex to be poured in.

Applying the plaster

You should mix only enough plaster to cover your model with one layer at a time, otherwise it will go off in the bowl before you have a chance to apply it. For a horse 31cm (12½in) high, you will require about

49 'Throwing' the plaster.

3.5kg (7½lb) of plaster and 2l (3½pt) of water for each plaster layer.

Mix the plaster as for the figure, on p. 31. It is advisable to place some newspaper on the working table and on the floor around the model during the next operation, as there could be some mess.

For the first application of plaster, remember that you are only casting one half of the mould. Hold the container in one hand, and with the other scoop out a handful of plaster. With the back of the hand held towards the model, throw the plaster from the ends of the fingers (see fig. 49). Enough force must be exerted to ensure that the plaster penetrates the smallest and finest detailed crevices. Plaster expands slightly on setting, further ensuring the penetration. The first layer of plaster must be about 10mm (⅜in) thick, and should still reveal the shape of the horse figure. The inside surface will now be a true copy of the original model, but it is much too thin to be removed. As this first layer begins to set, it should be gently roughened either with a spatula or with your finger. Small lumps of plaster could be added, making the surface as rough as possible so that it grips the second layer better. At this stage, enclose the horse model with a wooden frame, made roughly to the shape of the finished mould. The walls of the frame will determine the thickness and make storage easier by its squareness.

Prepare the plaster for the second layer in the same way as the first, but leave this mixture a little longer before applying it to the first layer so that it is a little harder or slightly 'going off'. Then throw the plaster on as before, until the full thickness of the clay band up to the wooden surrounding wall has been reached. This will act as a reinforcement, bringing the thickness up to the necessary 4cm (1½in) to carry the weight of the piece. Then, to facilitate storage, the outside wall can be smoothed off by running a piece of wood across the still-wet surface. When the plaster for the first half of the mould has set (in about 30 minutes), the wooden wall and the clay boundary bands and slips are removed, along with the soft, moistened paper which protected the uncast half of the clay model.

A word of warning before starting on the second half of the mould: do make sure that the keys are clearly indented in the plaster, that there are no air holes and that the wall is reasonably smooth. All these things can be corrected at this stage. If the keys are not clearly defined, then with the metal spatula penetrate into the plaster about 12mm (½in) making a hole about 25mm (1in) wide, funnel-shaped to allow for easier locking of the mould pieces. Air holes can be scraped and filled with mixed plaster, and the walls can be smoothed by scraping them with the metal spatula then rubbing them gently with sandpaper. All these repairs must be carried out without damaging the other half of the clay model.

Having satisfied yourself that all is in order, gently detach the iron upright from the base, fill in the small resulting cavity and

50 Cleaning up the inside of the plaster mould.

smooth off. The plaster walls should now be given a light wash of soapy water or a thin clay water wash; both act as a release agent to prevent plaster sticking to plaster.

Now make the second half of the mould in exactly the same way.

Removing the horse

After allowing the plaster to set for at least 30 minutes the mould is ready for opening. Take the 25mm (1in) chisel and gently prise the two halves of the mould slightly apart all the way round. On no account use undue force as this could damage the mould. Then, through the opening and using a half-filled

cup, allow a little water to penetrate. The water will find its way between the clay and the mould, causing the clay to swell and to push the two halves apart. It is then an easy matter to detach one piece of the mould from the clay. The other piece will still be attached to the clay model. Remove the clay surrounding the model and then take the model out. The remaining clay should come away easily. If there are any crevices where the clay cannot be reached with a brush, use a small modelling tool. Now, thoroughly clean the mould until all traces of clay have disappeared. Leave the two halves to dry out. As the casting is to be in latex, the surface of the mould must be free from all treatment.

51 Pouring the latex solution into the mould.

Casting

The finished mould is now ready for the next operation, that of pouring in the latex composition.

Reassemble the two halves of the mould, making sure that the keys fit snugly, and bind them together with a strong cord, making them fit closely one to the other. The cord should be taut around the mould, and if this is not possible with the cord alone, press in wedge-shaped pieces of wood between the cord and the plaster (see p. 42).

Turn the mould over with the hooves of the horse uppermost. These, with their funnel-shaped extensions, are the pour-holes. Balance the mould at an angle of 45 degrees, using the wedge-shaped piece of wood described on p. 42. Make the mixture 50 per cent liquid latex and 50 per cent filler paste. Mix these thoroughly and allow to stand for 24 hours for the air bubbles to disperse. Now continue to fill the mould and remove the completed cast horse according to the instructions for figures on p. 43.

Remove any flash lines with sandpaper and small files (fig. 53).

52 The two-piece mould, with registration keys.

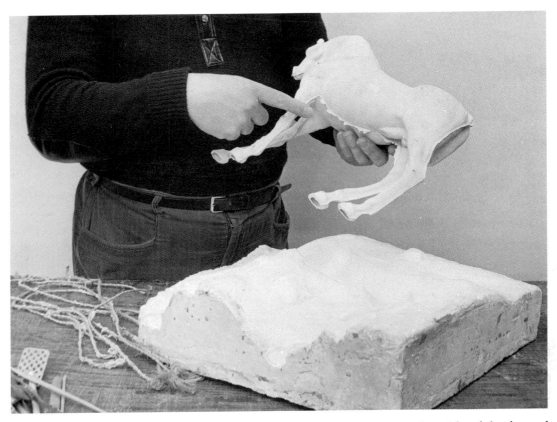

53 Remove the flash line with a knife and sandpaper or an electric buffing motor.

Accessories

The cavalry of the past were not, as one would expect, very good horsemen, and the control and training of the horses was achieved with a great deal of harshness. Most European armies used the *curb bit*. This was a piece of metal shaped into the figure H, the upright sides being called the 'branches', and in the centre was a bar with a shaped bend that varied considerably depending on the treatment given to the horse.

The *bridle* consisted of a crown piece that lay across the head just behind the ears and extended down on either side of the face of the horse. These extensions are called the cheek pieces. From just in front of the ears and attached on either side of the temple was the *browband*. The *cheek pieces* supported the *noseband* and the bit, which was held in the mouth of the horse. The hussar pattern of bridle had two extra straps which fastened cross-wise on the horse's face and was ornamented with a medallion. From the top of the cheek piece at the junction of the browband, a strap passed under the neck and fastened at the same point on the other side, this being known as the *throat latch*. The control of the horse was achieved by a chain which was attached to the upper ring of the bit where the cheek straps were attached and which ran from either side under the horse's chin. Attached to the lower branch of the bit was a rein known as

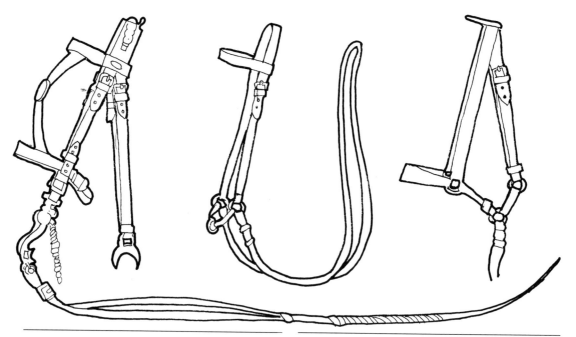

54 Three types of bridle.

55 Harness accessories: **a** bronzed American bit with ring; **b** a strap spur; **c** a screw-out neck spur; **d** a pistol belt of patent leather; **e** a cartridge box; **f** stirrup used by the American cavalry, 1860; **g** a stirrup as used by the Confederate Army, 1860.

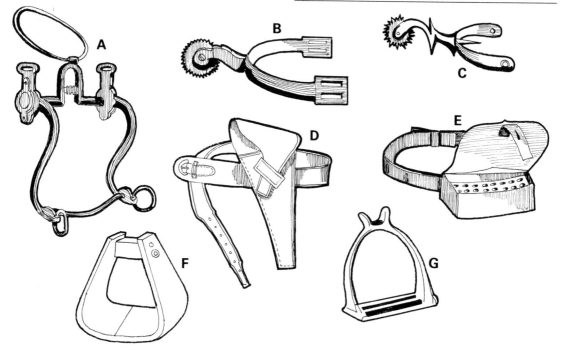

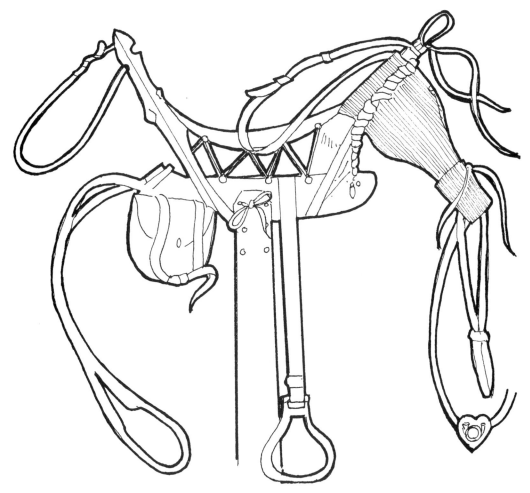

56 The Hussar saddle, as adapted for the Hungarians. Due to the lacing of the gaps between the side-bars with rawhide and stretched very tightly, the space along the spine of the horse was left completely free from the weight of the rider. The deep seat allowed the horseman to sit comfortably into the saddle.

the *curb rein* and by the rider pulling on this rein the U-shape on the bit turned and thrust the point or spade of the U-shape into the roof of the horse's mouth. The second rein, which was fastened on the upper branch of the bit, was called the *snaffle*. It was quite common practice for the cheek pieces, which were attached to the noseband, to be a different colour to the piece that fastened to the bit.

When assembling your accessories start with the strap holding any medallions or crescents; most hussar regiments had some form of ornamentation hanging from the throat latch. It was not uncommon for a cavalryman also to have a *martingale*. This was a strap that was fastened to the nose-band and to the saddle girth. Now place on the face pieces, the crown and cheek pieces, then the brow- and nosebands. All of these are made from leather thonging of various thicknesses, plus fuse wire for the bit.

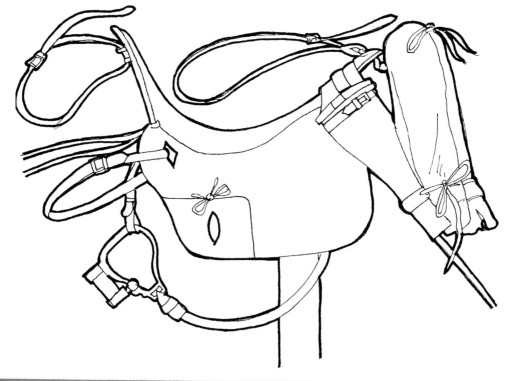

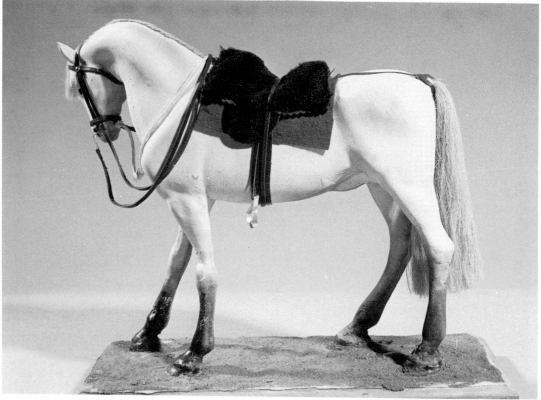

Left **57** The Lancer saddle, with a deep dip in the seat and high arches similar to the Hussar saddle. The high narrow 'spoon' rose from the centre of the cantel allowing a great deal of baggage to be carried. This type of saddle was adopted throughout Europe and America.

The *saddle* is either made from metal sheeting or modelled separately, and should fit as close as possible to the back but leave a clearance of the withers and along the length of the backbone. The *girth band* is placed in the sternum curb, which is just behind the elbows and is, to all intent and purpose, the horse's waistline. A *crupper strap* is also used to keep the saddle in position.

The *shabraque* is placed over the saddle and an additional girth strap is then fixed over and fastened to the saddle girth band. The *cantel* of the saddle comes through the aperture which is cut away on the shabraque. Sheep skins, if worn, are fastened on by straps around the pommel and the cantel of the saddle. Finally the *portmanteaux* and *blankets* are attached just behind the cantel.

Left **59** The finished horse complete with saddle and bridle.

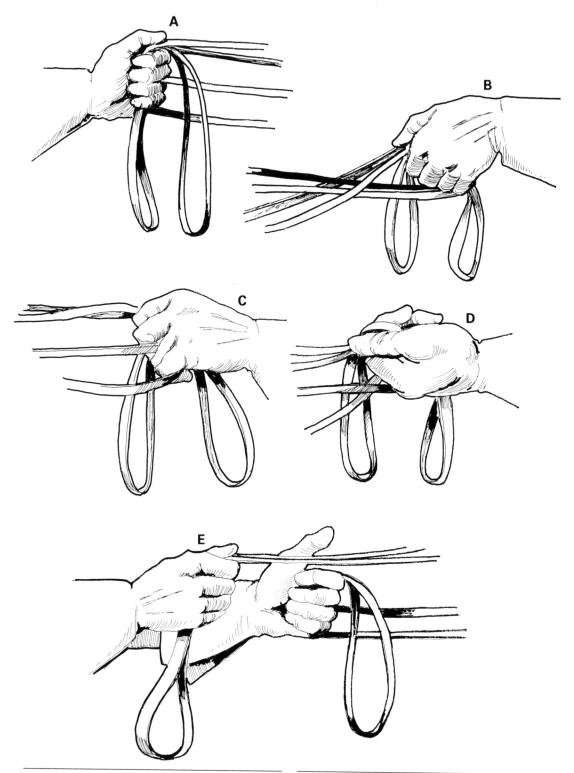

58 Positions of holding reins: **a** the pull on all four reins with the left hand; **b** the position of the curb rein (**x**) in use; **c** the knuckles of the hand in the low position showing the use of the curb rein; **d** the knuckles raised showing the pull of the near curb rein; **e** the reins separated.

8 Painting

The method of painting that I describe here has proved satisfactory for me over a number of years, but it is in no way to be assumed that this is the only method. I do not believe that there is any such thing as one perfect technique. I offer these instructions to show you the way to find your own method, the one that suits you and gives you the best results. Each one of us is, after all, an individual. We express our ideas and thoughts in a different way. All the models mentioned in this book can be painted using the method outlined below, whether they are large or small, in plastic, metal or latex.

60 Painting the main body, holding the model either by the base or by sticking on a small piece of dowelling and placing this inside a bottle.

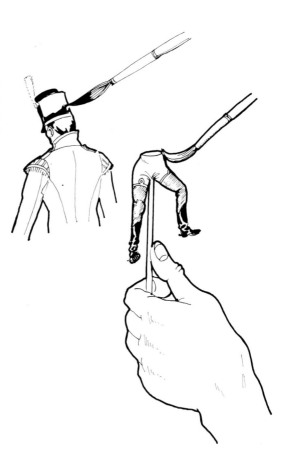

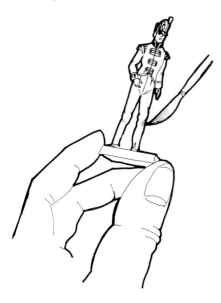

A

B

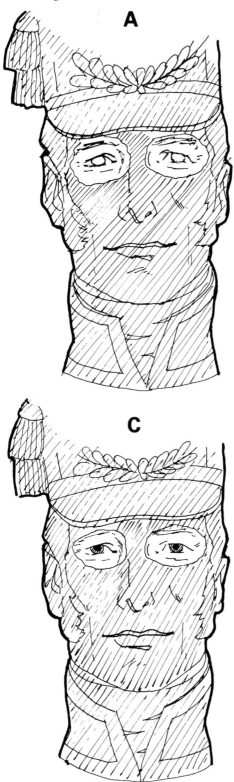

C

D

61 Stages in painting the face: **a** painting the sockets; **b** marking the irises; **c** placing the pupils in the centre of the irises; **d** the irises should be in line with the corners of the mouth; **e** adding burnt sienna; **f** bringing flesh colour to the eyes; **g** the eyebrows and hair.

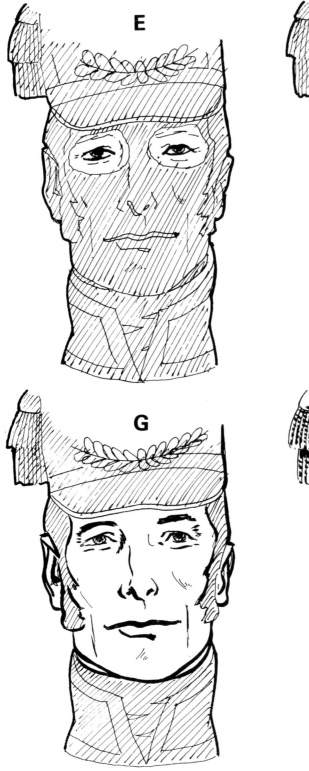

E

F

G

H

The face

Both oil paint and water-bound oil paint are suitable. On your working palette, lay out basic flesh colours: white, yellow and burnt sienna. Blending these together, you can get any shade of skin colouring, and no two people have the same. Make it a golden rule always to mix your flesh colours on a palette and never to paint straight from a tin.

The face must first of all be primed with a spray or a wash of white paint. Concentrate first on the eye area by giving it a coat of bluish white – rather more white than blue – covering the whole socket (fig. 61a). It is easier to bring the flesh colour around the eye area afterwards than the 'hit and miss' method of trying to dab a spot of white in the small space around the pupil. For the face, use three brushes: No. 3 for the heavy or mass area, No. 0 for the medium work and for all the very fine detail use a No. 00.

Having laid in the socket colour, paint with either burnt sienna or light blue a small circle in the centre of the eyeball for the irises (fig. 61b). With the No. 00 brush, and in direct line with the corners of the mouth as your guide, place a black dot in the centre of the blue or brown circle for the pupil (fig. 61c). Never attempt to put a white highlight in these very small eyes. It is usually fatal because it tends to give the eye a wild, angry stare. Mark out the upper and lower eyelids with burnt sienna mixed with just a touch of white to reduce the hardness (fig. 61e). Arch the upper lid line so that you cut the white of the eye down a little. This will give the eye a warmer look.

Now stop and study the eyes. Are they looking straight out at you? Do they appear cross-eyed, or worse, do they appear to wander to opposite corners? You can put right either of these faults now by whitewashing them out.

Next apply the flesh colour overall, bringing the flesh tone to the eyes themselves (fig. 61f). While the face paint is still wet, add a little more sienna with a spot of flesh colour, and apply shadow around the eyes, down either side of the nose and on the lip support (below the bottom lip) and under the chin. With a pure burnt sienna, line in the nostrils. With the paint still wet, the next operation is to texture the colour of the skin. Mix a spot of red with the basic flesh tint until you have a reddish pink. With this colour mark out the area just below the cheek bone, and blend in. Next apply the same reddish pink tone to the outer shape and centre of the ear and to the lips, adding a little more red to the upper lip. The separation line of the lips is best put in afterwards with a fine line of burnt sienna.

Examine your handiwork. Do you require to highlight the face, or is your modelling such that you have all the natural light and shade you require? If you do require highlights, you must mix more white with your basic flesh colour and apply this to the bridge of the nose, the ears and the cheeks and, if necessary, the chin. I do not recommend that you apply highlights to figures over 30cm (12in) high. Their features are large enough to be modelled; by natural light, such a figure can look very dramatic. The smaller figures, however, must have a certain build up both on their faces and their clothes.

When the face is dry, paint on the hair and the eyebrows in the colour of your choice – black, grey, red or brown – to denote the age or character of your model. Alternatively, fit your model with a wig.

A model of an N.C.O. in the 7th Regiment of Von Malackowsky Prussian Hussars, 1762.

A French *voltigeur* (skirmisher) of the 29th Infantry of Foot, in the uniform of 1809.

62 Field Marshal the Duke of Wellington
mounted on his favourite charger, Copenhagen.
Latex composition, 45cm (18in) high.

The hands

The hands are just as important as the face, so do not simply dab on flesh colour. Study them and apply dark and light shadows as required. The knuckles, which stand out a little, should be painted with just that extra touch of red mixed with the flesh tone. The shadows between the fingers should be the same colour as that used for the darker tone down the side of the nose. Burnt sienna should be used for the separation lines between the fingers. Highlights should appear along the leading edge of the fingers.

Clothes

The painting of clothes brings us to the next problem – that of achieving the look and feel of material. I usually strive to get the deadest of matt colours, although this does not apply to all materials. On the larger figures I always leave the modelled folds and creases to find their own light and shade. The smaller figures have to be helped along with the painting of the shadows and highlights.

The best way to give depth to the folds and creases on the smaller figures is to paint the clothes with the basic colour required, then mix a deeper hue of the same colour and apply to the shadow parts. When that is dry, line the innermost part of the shadow with a line of dark brown or black. Now mix a spot of white with the original basic colour and paint in the highlight on the top of the fold. To increase the depth of the folds, increase the highlight by using mainly white with just a touch of the basic colour paint on top. Study the old master paintings and you will discover many lighting tricks, especially on clothes.

A horse

I have used a wide range of materials for painting horses, from wood dye (which is very effective on latex models) to oil paint, and have been delighted with all my results.

A horse is painted in very much the same way as a figure. First of all, give it an undercoat of white. If your horse is to have a star or a blaze on its face these areas must be given an extra coat of white. Paint in the eyes dark brown, exposing little or no white, then paint in a black dot for the pupil. Fill in the nostrils and the muscle indentations with a darker colour than the overall colour of the horse. To give a realistic look to your horse, you must show the feathers (the long hair fat the back of the fetlocks) and the thinner-hair areas. The thinner-hair areas are the posterior parts, which are just in front of the hips on the flanks, on the breast or pectoral muscles between the legs and around the muzzle and the eyes. Paint these in a lighter colour and blend them into the main colour of the horse. The mane, if you paint this on rather than use nylon hair, should have streaks of lighter colours to give it a living, flowing quality. The legs can be finished off with some form of decoration such as white stockings or socks on the fetlocks.

For larger horses, nylon hair is essential for the mane and tail. Once it has been attached it can be cut, brushed, plaited, combed – in fact treated as if it were real.

9 Dioramas

The display of models is a combination of the detailed perfection of the model soldiers coupled with an authentic-looking background that together tell a story of an action long since past but, to the collector, a captured moment in time. With just two or three figures any collector can also tell a whole or part of a story. Depending on the size of the diorama within any limited area, you can make a diorama so that at all times it can be improved upon and extended, with each scene becoming just a piece in a large jigsaw. There must, therefore, be some prior planning to allow for each piece to become an action within itself and which in turn will become part of a greater action, until eventually a whole battle scene is completed. An impossible dream? Certainly not: each collector has the ability to achieve this. The idea is a simple one. Each base must be shaped according to the set plan and a simple locking piece fitted that will find a corresponding locking piece in the next scene.

Making the terrain

For each scene or diorama take a piece of wood 1.2cm (½in) thick, cut to shape according to the master plan (if you have one) and fit struts underneath to prevent warping. Then cover the surface with very small tacks, hammered in and then lightly bent over. These will be the keys to hold the papier mâché pulp, which will completely cover the diorama base.

The pulp, when made, is the most inexpensive form of modelling composition. It forms the perfect earth terrain contours and is the ideal building material for walls, rocks, cobblestones, dirt roads and parade-ground surfaces. The pulp is easy to make. Simply soak torn pieces of newspaper in a bowl of warm water (the soaking should be as long as possible, preferably overnight) and then rub between the hands to a pulpy condition. The pulp should be put through an ordinary household mincing machine if you have one (fig. 64b) as this will break up the pulp to a finer consistency. Form the pulp into a bowl shape, pour in some hot liquid glue size and mix these together. Then form this mixture into a bowl shape again, add plaster of Paris powder and mix together. The mixture will now be very malleable, a modelling composition that can be spread over the surface of the wooden base and shaped into the surface texture of the terrain required.

Once the terrain surface has been formed on the baseboard and before it is dry, you can sprinkle any of the textures available in model shops – sand, grass, moss, etc. depending on the effect you require. The

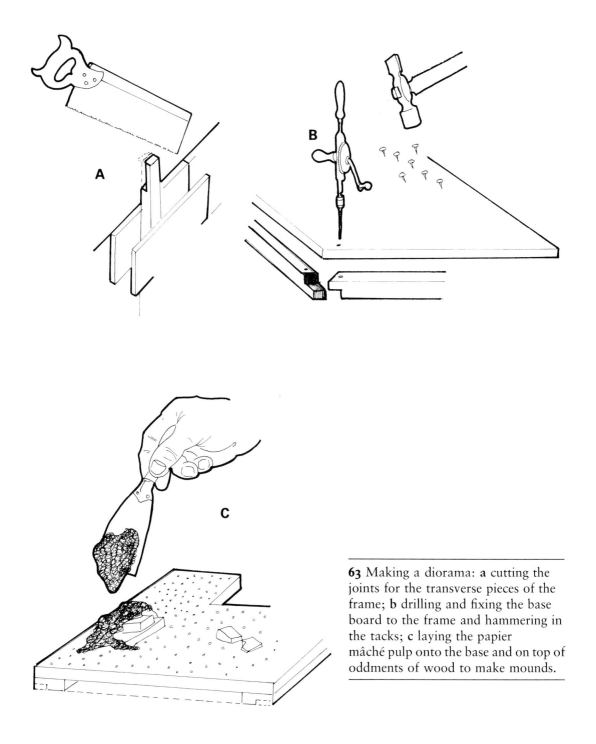

63 Making a diorama: **a** cutting the joints for the transverse pieces of the frame; **b** drilling and fixing the base board to the frame and hammering in the tacks; **c** laying the papier mâché pulp onto the base and on top of oddments of wood to make mounds.

64 Making papier mâché for a diorama:
a torn paper, ready to be soaked in water;
b feeding the mincing machine with wet and torn pieces of paper; **c** pouring the hot glue size into the paper pulp, then mixing together thoroughly.

task of smoothing in the terrain is a simple procedure of modelling, using a small glass of water and either a modelling spatula or your fingers. You can add ruts by running a gun or vehicle that is to be used in the diorama through the pulp mixture – make sure that you clean this carefully afterwards with a soft tissue. Once the basic ground is finished, but before the terrain is dry, you can build rocks and hills on simple foundations. Water effects can quite easily be built within the composition, either with glass or with a clear liquid plastic, available from most hardware shops. When the whole terrain is dry, paint it with suitable earthy colours using any type of paint. While the paint is still wet, you can strew coloured sawdust or sand over the surface. If a snow scene is required, a light paint over with white and then a sprinkle of white glitter will do the trick. This will adhere to both the wet paint and the pulp.

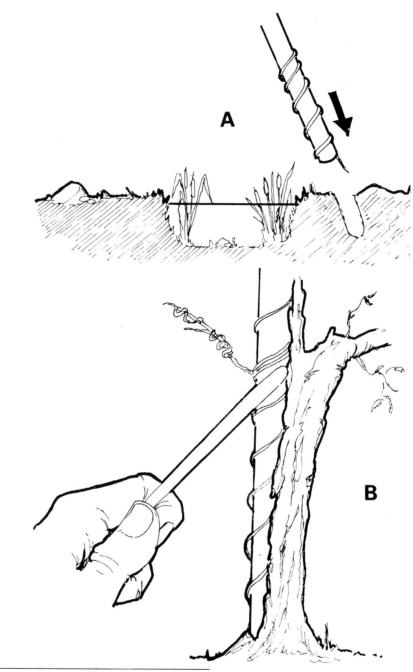

65 Modelling a tree: **a** planting a piece of
dowelling into a hole scooped out of the papier
mâché base; **b** modelling bark by building up
papier mâché on to the dowelling trunk and wire
branches.

Building up your scene

You can now start adding scenery, buildings and, of course, figures. Once you have decided on the positions of your soldiers, press them firmly into the pulp. This will hold them firmly.

Trees can be made by either covering a 12mm (½in) diameter dowel stick with small tacks or wrapping the dowel around with wire (fig. 65a). Lay papier mâché pulp on with a modelling tool (fig. 65b) and trace the bark effect over the surface. Add branches using twisted wire pieces extend-

ing from the main stem of the dowel stick, cover with pulp and model with the same effect as the tree. When dry, give them coats of brown and green paint.

If houses, buildings and sheds are to be used they should be built to last, so spend some time and effort in making them. Face the frames with a thin hardboard covered

66 Modelling a building: **a** a farmhouse frame; **b** the frame of a wall with the facing treated with papier mâché; **c** adding detail to a window frame using papier mâché.

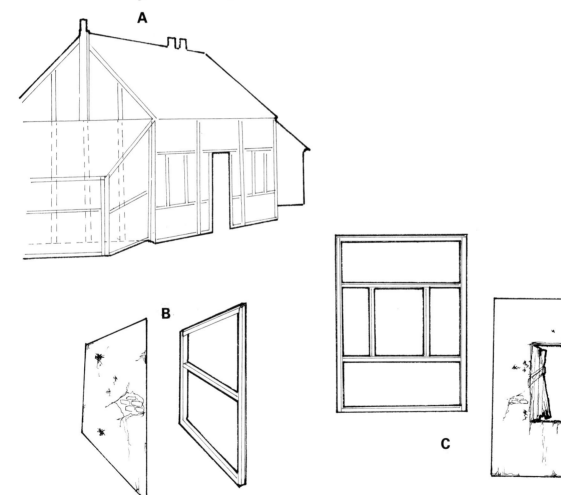

Left **67** Diorama of a battle scene depicting the Polish lancers of the Guard. The diorama is made from sand, and the illusion of depth is created by placing a 15cm (6in) model behind a 30cm (12in) model.

with a thin layer of pulp mixture, and mark out the surface with a modelling tool. Make frames for the roof sections and then cover with a peg-board hardboard. Sprinkle some more pulp mixture on and model the tiles. No great skill is required and when painted the effect is very professional. Books on older architectural buildings are a great asset if the action of the diorama calls for certain periods when the battle in question was fought within a city, town or village – there is nothing like authenticity to improve and put the finishing touches to your scene.

Loose roof tiles and cracked and broken walls showing shell and bullet holes look effective at the scene of a battle. These can all be made by modelling papier mâché onto pieces of wood or cardboard. Push the sharpened end of a pencil into the papier mâché where you want a bullet hole – you will find that the pulp is pushed out to look like highly realistic gun damage.

Glossary

Aiguillette shoulder strap of cord with a decorative knot and loops of plain or plaited cords fastening to a button

Armature wire wire used for forming the skeleton structure used to build clay models

Austrian knot similar to Hungarian knot, an ornamental cord design worn on cuffs and the front of trousers

Bandolier wide belt on which powder flasks and cartridge pouches were carried

Barrel belt a belt worn by hussar regiments; encircles the waist and ends in tassels

Baton ornamental military stick carried by officers

Bearskin large bearskin head-dress of fur worn by grenadiers

Bicorne a two-pointed hat with the points usually to the front and back

Bonnet de Police the name used for a French soldier's forage or fatigue cap

Brandenburgs decorative lace or cord linking two buttons

Breeches tight fitting trousers

Brown Bess the standard British musket from 1730 until the beginning of the nineteenth century.

Burnous cloak with sleeves of varying lengths and a hood

Busby fur head-dress, smaller than a bearskin, worn by hussars, usually with a cloth bag falling to one side

Cap soft head-dress of varying shapes, sometimes with a peak

Carbine a short musket used mainly by cavalry

Cartouche a small pouch worn on the shoulder belt

Chevrons lace denoting rank

Chin scales metal scales on a leather backing, fastened from the helmet and tied under the chin

Cockade a rosette in the national colours of the country

Colpack a round fur busby, often with a flap at the top hanging down one side

Contra-epaulette epaulette without fringes

Cross belts worn to carry the cartridge pouch, ammunition pouch, bayonet and sword

Cutaway kind of tail coat with the fronts curving away slightly

Dolman hussar-type, tight-fitting jacket

Epaulette shoulder strap with fringes

Facings parts of a uniform such as collar, cuffs and lapels which are in the colours of the regiment, different from the main colour of the uniform
Figure iron iron support for building models
Flintlock type of musket of which the lock had a flint
Flounders flat, oval woven decorations usually hanging from the hat or shoulder
Fob chain suspended from the waist, which carried the seal or a watch
Frock coat originated in the eighteenth century for informal wear, eventually became the undress uniform

Gaiters a covering cloth or leather for the ankles and lower legs; fastened mainly at the side
Gauntlets gloves with stiffened tops

Hanger sword a short sword carried by the infantry
Hungarian knot intricate braiding of interwoven circles on the thighs of hussar type breeches
Hussar boots made of soft leather curving up at the front and back with a 'V' notch with sometimes a tassel at the front

Khaki from the Persian word meaning dust or ashes
Kurta loose-type blouse, reaching the knees, with an opening at the front to the waist

Lance long wooden shaft with a pointed steel head from 3 to 5.5m (10 to 18ft) long, often carrying a pennant at the head

Mirliton tall cone-shaped peakless head-dress with a spiral cloth wound round
Mitre stiffened hat rising to a peak, often richly embroidered

Overalls long trousers with a strap under the boots

Pectoral decorative part of a horse harness
Pelisse fur-trimmed coatee worn by hussars, usually slung over the left shoulder
Pickelhaube German spiked helmet
Pickers small pins used to clean the touch-hole of a firearm
Piping raised edge around the collar, cuffs, jacket, pockets, seams, etc.
Plastron front of a uniform, sometimes fastened back to display the facing colours
Pom-pon a round worsted wool ball worn on headgear in place of a plume

Registration keys holes and matching cavities to ensure both halves of a mould fit together accurately
Riding breeches breeches with extra width given over the thighs, giving them their characteristic shape

Sabre sword with curved blade

Sabretache plain or embroidered flat bag attached by two or three slings to the sword belt

Sam Browne belt used to support the sword from a waistbelt, named after General Sir Samuel Browne

Sash band of material worn from right shoulder to left hip, or around the waist with hanging or tasseled ends either at the back or side

Shako a peaked rigid head-dress either cylindrical or bell-topped

Shoulder straps cloth shoulder pieces fastening near the collar, originally meant for keeping shoulder belts from slipping

Slash cuff or coat ornamentation, usually with buttons

Spatula flat wooden or metal modelling tool

Sword knot strap worn around the wrist to the hilt of the sword to prevent its loss in action

Tricorne a three-pointed hat replaced by the bicorne towards the end of the eighteenth century

Turban Persian word meaning veil material from which the Persians made the tightly-tied close-fitting head-dress; the Arabs and other Eastern countries also adopted the turban

Turnbacks tails of the coat folded and fastened back to reveal the lining or facing colour. Later they became sham and were sewn into place, being purely ornamental

Suppliers

Many of the materials required to make the models and accessories are available either from model shops or oddments that you may well have around the house already. The suppliers listed below are particularly good for stocking some of the more unusual items mentioned.

Britain

Bellman Carter (86) Ltd, rear of 358 Grand Drive, London SW20 (*plaster, latex and general hardware*)

Brodie & Middleton Ltd, 68 Drury Lane, London WC2 (*latex, rubber, paints, etc.*)

Strand Glass Fibre, Brentway Trading Estate, Brentford, Middx. (*moulding rubber and casting materials*)

Alec Tiranti, 70 High Street, Theale, Reading, Berks, (*moulding rubber and casting materials*)
    Also at: 27 Warren Street, London W1 (*as above plus sculptors' tools*)

Tradition Military Models, 5a Shepherd Street, London W1 (*models and books*)

Under Two Flags, 4 St Christopher Place, London W1 (*models and books*)

America

A.B.C. Hobby Craft, 2156 E. Moran Ave., Evansville, IN 47711 (*general*)

Black & Co., Hardware Hobby Shop, 8th S. Monroe, Springfield, IL 62702 (*general*)

Contact Inc., 9 Elm Street, Hudson, NH 03051 (*resistance soldering outfits*)

Craftsmen Speciality Supply, 6608 Forty Mile Point, Rogers City, MI 49779 (*metal, wood, plastics and castings*)

Hobby Chest Inc., 615 Howard Street, Evanston, IL 60202 (*general*)

Hobby World, 3120 Platt Springs Road, W Columbia, SC 29169 (*general*)

I.S.L.E. Laboratories Inc., 10009 E. Toldeo Road, Blissfield, MI 49228 (polyurethane foam and latex casting materials)

Polks Hobby Department Store, 314 Fifth Avenue, 32nd Street, NY1 (*general*)

The Old Guard, 33 Main Street, New Hope, PA 18938 (*general*)

The Soldier Centre, P.O. Box 38, West Roxbury, MA 02132 (*general*)

Imrie/Risley Miniatures, 425a Oak Street, Copiague, NY 11726 (*general*)

Valley Plaza Hobbies, 12160 Hamlin Street, CA 91606 (*general*)

Bibliography

Alberini, M., *Model Soldiers*, Orbis, 1973

Asquith, Stuart, *Military Modelling Guide to Wargaming*, Argus Books, 1987

Blum, Peter, *Model Soldiers: A Basic Guide to Painting, Animation & Conversion*,
  Arms and Armour, 1971

Blum, Peter, *Model Soldier Manual*, Imrie-Risley, New York, 1971

Blum, P. & Stearns, P., *Military Miniatures*, Hamlyn, 1965

Carman, W. Y., *Model Soldiers*, Arms & Armour 1969, Charles Letts & Co. 1973

Chesnau, Roger, *Scale Models in Plastic*, Conway Maritime Press, 1979

Dilley, Roy, *Scale Model Soldiers*, Almark, 1972

Dilley, Roy & Fosten, Bryan, *Dioramas & Scenic Settings*, Almark, 1977

Dixey, Graham, *The Art of the Model Soldier*, Argus Books, 1988

Ellis, Chris, *Advanced Plastic Modelling*, Patrick Stephens, 1970
  How to go Plastic Modelling, Patrick Stephens, 1970
  How to Build Plastic Kits, Ballantine, New York, 1973

Featherstone, D., *Military Modelling*, Kaye & Ward, 1970

Garratt, John G., *Model Soldiers for the Connoisseur*, Weidenfeld & Nicholson, 1973
  Model Soldiers for the Collector, New York Graphic Society 1972
  Model Soldiers: A Collector's Guide, Seeley Service & Co., 1971

Goodenough, Simon, & Tradition, *Military Miniatures*, Orbis, 1977

Harris, H., *Model Soldiers*, Octopus, 1972

Jackson, A. & Day, D., *Modelmaker's Handbook*, Pelham Books 1981

Jones, Ken, *Military Modelling Guide to Military Modelling*, Argus, 1987

Quarrie, B (Ed.) *Modelling Miniature Figures*, Patrick Stephens 1975

Paine, Sheperd, *How to Build Dioramas*, Kalmach Books, 1988 (USA)

Richards, W. *Old British Model Soldiers 1893–1918*, Arms & Armour 1970

Risley, C. A., & Imrie, *The Model Soldier Guide*, Imrie/Risley New York 1965

Smeed, V. (Ed.) *Encyclopedia of Military Modelling* Octopus 1981 & Peerage 1985

Stearns, Philip, *How to make Model Soldiers*, Hamlyn, 1974

Windrow M. & Embleton, G., *Model Soldiers*, Patrick Stephens, 1981

Index